Catering:

Housekeeping and Front Office

Companion volume to *Catering: Food Preparation and Service*

Ursula Jones

MHCIMA Cert. Ed.
Department of Catering and Hairdressing
Tresham College

Illustrations by Norman Laing NDD, ATD,
Former Head of Department, Tresham College

Hodder & Stoughton

LONDON SYDNEY AUCKLAND TORONTO

© 1986 Ursula Jones

First published in Great Britain 1986
Second impression 1989

British Library Cataloguing in Publication Data

Jones, Ursula
    Catering : housekeeping and front office.
    1. Caterers and catering—Vocational
    guidance—Great Britain
    I. Title
    647′.95′02341   TX911.3.V62

    ISBN 0–7131–7494–3

Printed in Great Britain for the educational publishing
division of Hodder and Stoughton Ltd, Mill Road, Dunton
Green, Sevenoaks, Kent by Page Brothers (Norwich) Ltd.

Contents

Catering: Food Preparation and Service
The contents of this companion volume include: Catering Methods and Equipment; Beverages and Light Meals; Soups, Sauces, Farinaceous Foods and Vegetables; Fruits and Pastry Work; Dairy Produce; Fish and Meats; Nutrition and Foods; Hygiene and Catering Premises; Food Service; and Food and Beverage Control.

Preface

This book has been written to fill an obvious need for a basic theory book that is in an easily read format to encourage all students who have experienced difficulty with comprehension of the written word. The extensive use of flow charts, diagrams, tables and illustrations is intended to increase the students' ability to understand and learn the theory element of any craft/skill-based course of study.

The book has been written for those students who are in any way interested in or studying catering and hospitality, either at their place of work, at a college of further education or at school. It has been designed so that any topic being studied is easily found and so that relevant information, charts and illustrations are adjacent to the main text. Much of the information has been included in list or chart form to minimise the amount of written text.

To help teachers there are questions in the form of assessment activities, which will extend the students' knowledge and their ability to apply this to their place of work or training. These activities have been designed so that the students may work as individuals or with two or three other students to form small study groups.

Students studying craft/skill-based courses examined by the City and Guilds London Institute will find the contents relevant to examinations 705, 708, 709 and the 700 skill-based series, and to accommodation studies for BTEC diploma students. Trainees studying CPVE, TVEI, HCITB, vocational preparation and YTS craft-proficiency training courses will find the book helpful and relevant to their training.

It is hoped that many students will find the contents of this book interesting, useful and easy to understand. The subject – catering – conjures up all manner of different types, sizes, styles and standards of establishment and service. I have endeavoured to give readers an indication of the many principles involved, thereby equipping them to study any part of the catering and hospitality industry in more depth as their careers and studies progress.

This book also contains basic information relevant to housekeeping and hotel reception services, and its companion volume, *Catering: Food Preparation and Service*, contains information concerned with food products, food production and food service, and the control of catering premises. These two books are intended to provide the necessary basic theoretical knowledge for catering hospitality students and should be used in conjunction with one another, together with practical skill instruction.

Acknowledgements

Thanks to my family and friends for their support and encouragement during the preparation of this book. The publishers would like to thank the following for their permission to reproduce copyright material: Access for the Access card illustration, Barclays Bank for banking material; British Gas for 'Help Yourself to Gas Safety'; The Banking Information Service for information from 'Sample bank cards, forms and documents'; Contico Manufacturing Limited for their advertisement; 'Laundry & Cleaning News International' for their illustrations; Merricks Sico Limited for their advertisement; The Royal Lancaster Hotel for their brochure; Stanley Thornes (Publishers) Ltd for a diagram from Jones & Phillips: *Commercial Housekeeping and Maintenance*; Truvox Floorcraft Ltd for their advertisement; and Vingcard Systems (UK) Ltd for illustrations.

Unit 1:

Residential Establishments

Types of residential establishment

The following table gives details of the facilities offered by various residential establishments, and lists staff and their specific duties.

Type	Facilities	Key housekeeping staff and duties
Seaside hotel (in summer)	Full/part board. Children's play area. Babysitters. Clothes-drying area. Restaurants/bars. Entertainments.	Housekeeper — control of housekeeping department. Room-maids — cleaning and room service to bedroom. Cleaners — cleaning of public areas. Linen-room staff — care and control of linen.
Seaside hotel (out of summer season)	Conference facilities. Weekend 'breaks'. Group bookings. Exhibitions, meetings. Restaurants/bars. Entertainments.	Head housekeeper — control of all housekeeping. Assistant housekeeper — all housekeeping in one section; helps housekeeper. Room-maids — cleaning and service of bedrooms. Cleaners — cleaning of public areas. Linen-room staff — care and control of linen.
Small town or country hotel	Weekly terms. Casual trade. Restaurant and bars. Car-parking area.	Manageress/housekeeper — deputy manager, control and running of all the housekeeping department. Room-maids/cleaners — cleaning and service of bedrooms and public rooms.
Motel	Open 24 hours per day. Restaurant and bars. Chalet accommodation. Car-park, and petrol sales. Coffee shop.	Manageress or housekeeper — running of the accommodation department. Daily cleaners — cleaning of all chalets and public areas.
City hotel	Restaurants and bars. Cocktail lounge. Private suites. Conference facilities. Meeting rooms. Coffee shop. Garage and car-parking. Group bookings. Weekend 'breaks'.	Head housekeeper — control of housekeeping department. Assistant housekeepers — control of an area of the hotel housekeeping department. Room-maids — service and cleaning of bedrooms. Cleaners — cleaning of public rooms and staff rooms and areas.

Type	Facilities	Key housekeeping staff and duties
	Shops. Health club. Sauna. Gymnasium. Barbers.	House porter − moving of heavy items, linen, refuse, high cleaning, e.g. windows. Florist − provision and arrangement of flowers. Valet − pressing and cleaning of guests' clothes.
Hostel, YMCA, YWCA	Bed-sitting room accommodation. Communal lounges and dining rooms. Utility rooms.	Warden/manager − control and care of the whole hostel and of the residents. Cleaners − cleanliness of the whole hostel.
Hall of residence	Single study-bedrooms. Cafeteria/self-catering facilities. Common rooms. Bars. Utility rooms.	Warden − complete control of all residents. Domestic bursar − control of the building and its up-keep. Assistant domestic bursars − supervision of the cleanliness of the facilities. Cleaners − cleanliness of all areas.
School boarding houses	Dormatories/shared bedrooms. Communal dining and lounge facilities. TV room. Games room. Study rooms.	Housemistress −may be housemaster's wife, has control of housekeeping section. Matron − welfare of pupils. Linen-room staff − care of linen and pupils' clothes and uniform. Cleaners − cleanliness of premises.
Hospital	*Patients:* wards and day-rooms. Specialist treatment rooms/areas. *Staff:* Nurses' homes. Doctors' flats. Recreation facilities. Lounges, restaurants.	Domestic services manager − responsible for cleanliness of a group of hospitals. Domestic superintendents − responsible for one large or two small hospital units. Assistant domestic superintendents − responsible for a section of a hospital. Domestic supervisor − cleanliness of an area of the hospital. Domestic assistants − cleaning of the hospital. Linen-room staff − cleanliness of all linen.

Type	Facilities	Key housekeeping staff and duties
Cruise liner	Luxury cabins with bathroom/suite of rooms. Lounges. Restaurants. Bars. Cinemas. Shops. Beauty/barber shops. Laundry/valet service. Entertainments. Swimming/sports facilities. Sauna baths. Jacuzzi. Gymnasium. Medical/doctor services.	Chief Steward – responsible for the cleanliness of the ship and the smooth running of all customer services. Control of staff. Stewards – customer services in all departments. Cabin maids – cleanliness of cabins. Cleaners – cleanliness of passenger areas. Laundry staff – care of all linen and customer laundry services.
Holiday camp	Chalet accommodation. Self-catering/full board. Entertainments of all types – sports facilities, swimming facilities.	Manager (accommodation) – responsible for all accommodation and staff. Chalet maids – cleanliness of chalets. Cleaners – cleanliness of all public areas.

The housekeeper

The housekeeper is responsible to the management of the establishment for the efficient and smooth running of the department. Such a position calls for special qualities of character, a personality that is capable of dealing and working with other people, and a varied experience of residential work. A large part of a housekeeper's day brings her into contact with both staff and guests. Honesty, good manners, cheerfulness, self-control, tact, patience and a quiet, efficient manner are qualities that will help to make a successful housekeeper.

In general, the housekeeper will be responsible for the following sections of work within her department:

- Liaison with other departments.
- Checking and reporting on the cleanliness and maintenance of all areas of the establishment.
- Staff selection and training, supervision, and duty rostas.
- Guest comfort and welfare.
- Control and maintenance of linen stocks.
- Promotion of safe practice and working conditions.
- Provision of first aid to guests and staff.
- Control and maintenance of housekeeping stores and equipment.
- The keeping of departmental records.

4

- The promotion of clean, pleasant premises and the provision of floral decorations.

Incidents that the housekeeper will normally deal with include the following:

- If a guest complains about his or her allocated room, because of either the furnishings or exterior-noise nuisance, the housekeeper or the duty manager should be informed at once. The housekeeper or the duty manager will investigate the cause of complaint, and authorise a change of room if this is considered appropriate.
- If a guest falls ill, the housekeeper should be informed at once. A doctor will then be sent for, if necessary. The housekeeper will supervise the supply of extra bedding, refreshments, the sending of messages and the collection of purchases, either before or after the doctor's visit.
- If a guest wishes to have his family sleeping in his room, the housekeeper will supervise the supply and fixing up of a cot and/or a child's bed, or a room with a communicating door to an adjacent bedroom may be suggested to the guest, in which case the housekeeper will ensure that the door between the two rooms is left unlocked when the guest and his family take possession of the two rooms.

Housekeeping responsibility

The housekeeping responsibility may include some or all of the following areas:

Exterior	Internal/front house	Back/house
Patio area.	Reception area/foyer.	Staff accommodation area.
Roof-top garden.	Restaurant.	Offices.
Veranda.	Coffee shop.	Kitchens.
Outside restaurant.	Retail shop.	Service rooms.
Loading bay.	Lifts/staircases.	Store-rooms.
Underground car-park.	Lounge.	Cellar.
Covered walkway.	Bedrooms.	Service lifts.
Swimming-pool area.	Conference area.	Linen-room.
Outdoor sports area.	Cloakrooms.	Fire-escapes.
Porch area and balcony.	Licensed bar.	

Factors that may affect the room-maid's daily work include the following:

- Group bookings all arriving and departing at the same time.
- Group bookings all going to see/visit sights at the same time.
- Delays with supplies of linen or cleaning equipment.
- Damage or breakages in the room to be cleaned.

- 'Do not disturb' requests on bedroom doors.
- Group of 'late risers' which delays the room-maid's work.
- Early relets for use during the day.
- Suites used for meetings during the day.

Guest-room supplies may include all or some of the following:

- 'Do not disturb' notices.
- Continental breakfast request/order cards.
- Early morning tea request cards.
- Ashtrays and book matches.
- Shoe-shine pads.
- Room-service menus.
- Hotel information cards.
- In-house magazines.
- Printed stationery and pens.
- Gideon Bible.
- Telephone directories.
- Coat hangers.
- Laundry bags and cards.
- Soap and shampoo.
- Shower caps.
- Facial tissues.
- Emergency repair sewing-kit.
- Disposable bath mat.

Some rooms in hotels offer a guest the facilities to make his/her own cup of tea or coffee. The equipment in the room will include the following:

- An electric kettle.
- Cups, saucers and spoons.
- Individual cartons of UHT milk.
- A teapot.
- Sachets of tea and instant coffee.
- Sugar cubes and biscuits.

Staffing structures

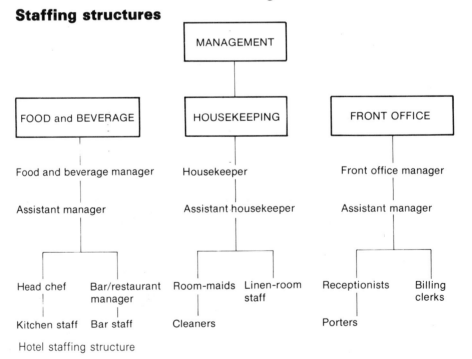

Hotel staffing structure

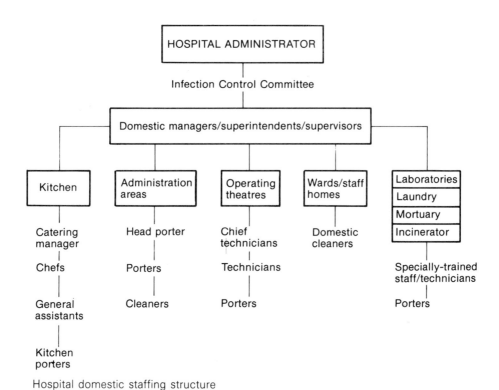

Hospital domestic staffing structure

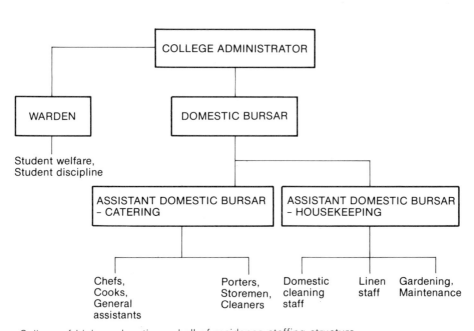

College of higher education – hall of residence staffing structure

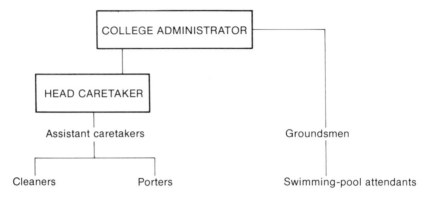

Tuition/teaching area domestic staffing structure

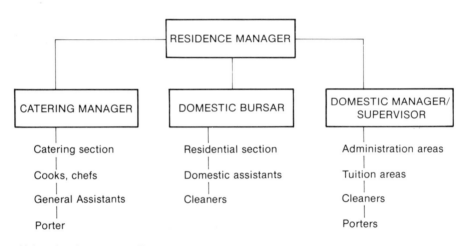

University domestic staffing structure

Shops

The area used for shops may be leased to local or national retail companies, who will undertake to use the area to retail an agreed selection/range of products to the hotel guests and to members of the public.

These shops may arrange for the sale of the following:

- Clothing, sports wear, leisure wear and footwear.
- Chemist – toiletries and cosmetic items.
- Souvenir and craft items.
- Jewellery – often locally designed and made.

- Banking and postal facilities.
- Business/secretarial facilities for typing, recording business meetings, writing letters and taking business messages.

If the hotel or cruise-liner has a sports and health club complex, there is likely to be a sports and leisure-wear shop adjacent to this facility. Shops of this type are usually situated near the foyer of the hotel, or on one of the upper-level decks between the class barriers on cruise-liners. All shops serve the purpose of increasing revenue to the management of the hotel or liner, as well as providing additional amenities for the guests and the staff, especially if on a liner or in an isolated area.

Kiosks

These are generally run by the management of the liner or hotel, which ensures that there is complete control over the standard and type of service offered. There is also more control over the range and price of goods offered for sale. The management may select its own staff to run these kiosks, and have flexible trading hours to suit the requirements of the residents. It is also in a position to promote local events in the area, as and when this is appropriate. The type of items often sold in these small retail outlets are as follows:

- Daily, local, and national and international newspapers and periodicals.
- Stationery and writing materials (pens and pencils).
- Items for children's amusement, such as puzzle books and games.
- Souvenirs, confectionery and chocolates.
- Maps, guidebooks, postcards of local beauty spots.
- Cosmetics and toiletries.

Telephone coin-boxes

These are often located in the same area as the shops and kiosks, so that the guests may use all the facilities. A guest wishes to use the telephone and, while doing so, may decide to go into one or more of the shops. This is a hidden form of advertising the facility, and it should not be overlooked when planning kiosks and shops.

Coffee shops in hotels

These are provided to enable the guests to obtain beverages and snacks at any time of the day and evening. This facility relieves pressure on both the main restaurants and the room-service facilities.

Purpose
- To provide a retail area for the sale of beverages, such as tea and coffee.
- To provide complete meals that may be selected from an individually priced menu.

Features
- Normally run with waiter service in a less formal style than is found in the main restaurants, with an attractive display of foods in a heated/chilled area and a sweet-trolley.
- Open every day, all day and evening.
- May have access directly outside to encourage members of the general public to use the facility and thereby see the inside of the hotel. This provides indirect advertising.
- There should be attractive, cheerful decor and fittings, with facilities for guests of all ages and tastes.
- There should be adequate space for briefcases, umbrellas and light hand-luggage.
- If the hotel is situated near a railway terminal or an airport, there will be a huge trade for passengers' refreshment between stages of their journey.

Vending in hotels

Situations where vending may be advantageously used include the following:

Public
- Bedroom landings for alcoholic beverages and mixers.
- Bars for cigarettes and confectionery.
- Foyer area for postage stamps, postcards, books, periodicals, sweets and chocolate.
- Cloakrooms for toiletries.

Staff
- Rest-rooms for beverages, cold drinks, confectionery, light snacks and cigarettes.

Advantages of vending	Disadvantages of vending
Cost control; cash control; stock control; items always available, especially at night; low staff costs for filling and cleaning; may be leased with an option on a contract for stock supply and replenishing.	Attractive to vandals; can look unsightly; may make an unpleasant noise and tend to encourage litter; some guests do not like using vending machines; foreign coins can cause breakdowns.

Give-away products

These products are purchased by the hotel, airliner or cruise-liner, and may be embossed with the company logo. Sometimes the name, address and telephone number of the company is included. These items are a form of indirect advertising, as guests and customers are encouraged to take them home as souvenirs. They may also have the advantage of reducing pilferage of ashtrays, tea-spoons and other small items which frequently go missing.

Give-away products include the following types of gift:

General	Housekeeping
Book or box of matches.	Soap tablets.
Sachets of chocolates.	Sachets of shampoo.
Drink drip-mats.	Sachets of bath oil.
Sachets of sugar.	Shower caps.
Cigarettes or cigars.	Sewing kits.
Calendars.	Notepaper and envelopes.
Decorated cocktail sticks.	Postcards.
Magazines.	Pencils and pens.
Tourist guides or maps.	Notepads.

Arrangements of fresh fruit and flowers are occasionally placed in a hotel suite or room for the guests' enjoyment and as a means of welcoming them to the hotel. This method of welcome is greatly appreciated by guests but is costly for the management.

Customer satisfaction

This is difficult to evaluate but there are signs, which staff can be trained to recognise, that will give an indication of customers' appreciation of the services.

Positive signs	Negative signs
1 Guests look happy and pleased.	1 Guests look unhappy and sullen.
2 They talk pleasantly to the staff.	2 They snap at the staff and raise their voices.
3 They make enquiries about future bookings or visits.	3 They give no indication of planning future visits.
4 They walk at a leisurely pace in a relaxed manner.	4 They tend to hurry around in a tense manner.
5 They eat and drink in a quiet, easy manner.	5 They eat and drink in a quick – maybe even aggressive – manner.

Bedrooms

Depending on the type of establishment, bedrooms may vary as follows:

Boarding school	Hall of residence
Purpose: to provide safe, easily cleaned, pleasant room suitable for young persons. **Fittings**: single beds, up to six per dormatory; space for pupils' clothes; strong furniture; bed-side lockers for personal belongings; emulsion walls. **Special**: pupils resident during term-time; may be very young; safety is a prime concern; tidy own rooms.	**Purpose**: to provide quiet, peaceful, attractive room for studying and sleeping. **Fittings**: hand-basin; pin-board; strong bed; book shelves; desk and chair; cupboards for clothes; strong, easily cleaned carpet and furniture; emulsion walls. **Special**: permanent residents per academic year; change own bed linen and tidy own room; conference trade in vacations.
General hotel	Luxury hotel
Purpose: to provide quiet, clean, comfortable room with attractive decor. **Fittings**: divan beds; hand-basin, or bathroom en suite; wardrobe and a drawer unit; luggage rack; lamp; telephone; radio and television; carpet, and wallpaper on walls. **Special**: high standards of cleanliness required; good security for guests' personal property.	**Purpose**: to provide peaceful, well-appointed spacious room, with attractive furnishings. **Fittings**: Bathroom en suite; divan beds of good size; arm-chairs; coffee table; radio and television; telephone; luxury decor; space for clothes and luggage; personal safe; mini bar/refrigerator; good view; flowers. **Special**: air conditioning; room service; exceptionally high standards of service and cleanliness required.
Cruise-liner cabins	Trains – compartments
Purpose: to provide comfortable sleeping accommodation while cruising. **Fittings**: all items permanently fixed to eliminate movement; space for all personal belongings; compact units; air conditioning; hand-basin, or bathroom en suite. **Special**: high standard of cleanliness required; good security.	**Purpose**: to provide sleeping accommodation for passengers travelling overnight. **Fittings**: bunk beds fold down from seats used during day-time travel; small hand-basin and minimum hanging space for clothes; very compact area; blinds on door; individual lights per bunk. **Special**: stewards board train to prepare compartments for sleeping.

Hospital ward

Purpose: to provide hygienic, safe, comfortable area in which patients can be treated by medical staff and which remains cheerful and pleasant.
Fittings: all surfaces are impervious and easily cleaned; beds, lockers and bed-trays are on castors; arm-chairs and foot-stools are made of washable materials; washable curtains and screens; emulsion walls; sealed floor surfaces, with non-slip finish; central heating; hand-basins.
Special: a lack of harmful bacteria is the prime concern; the atmosphere created must be conducive to the patients' well-being and comfort.

Flower arrangements

When using flowers or plants inside a residential building the following principles should be followed:

Flowers

- The flowers and container should be in proportion; tall containers need flowers that are twice the height of the vase.
- Always use dark colours and shades at the base of the arrangement and lighter shades at the top.
- Choose colours that will blend into the surroundings; remember that flowers are intended to enhance the finished appearance of the room.
- Large arrangements may be placed upon a stand-table or shelf at strategic points for instant effect.
- A mirror behind or beneath an arrangement can create an attractive effect, and can increase the light reflected on to the area.
- Spotlights and wall-lights may be used to increase the flowers' effect.
- For tables, a small, low arrangement will be more acceptable than a spreading arrangement, especially if food is being served.
- Highly perfumed flowers can be attractive in large, public areas but may be considered to be unacceptable if placed upon dining tables or in very confined areas.
- Flowers will thrive in cool areas, but if they are allowed to become too warm their life will be considerably shortened.
- The base and container should be stable and well balanced to eliminate any accidents caused by sudden draughts or jolts.
- The finished shape of the arrangement should be suitable for the size and position of the arrangement within that room.

Plants

- These will have a much longer life than cut flowers and may be used in single pots or placed in complementary groups to give a variety of leaf colour, shape and texture, as well as a variety of flower colour.

- Plants may be interchanged between different areas within the same establishment to lengthen their life and to create changes within rooms. This will also help to promote even growth of the plants.
- Conservatories, verandas and patios are often furnished so that the use of plants is appropriate and attractive.
- Plants should be moved regularly to ensure that they are healthy, growing evenly and are not becoming infested with insects or flies.
- Potted plants may be in groups planted in one large trough or pot to allow greater variety and effect. This will provide a semi-permanent display, suitable for entrance halls, foyers and reception areas.

The therapeutic value of flowers and plants should be fully recognised in hospitals, and especially when units are concerned with patients' rehabilitation. Plants may be cultivated by these patients and then used in the rest of the hospital, with considerable benefit to all the patients.

Room interior effects

Relief to interiors is provided by one or more of the following: potted plants, flowers, pictures, sculptures, photographs, maps, display cabinets and illumination.

Flowers

Live cut flowers are used as displays as previously described, but they have a limited life. This has caused the extensive use of silk or fabric imitation flowers, to create semi-permanent displays. These are very realistic and are acceptable alternatives to real flowers in many areas.

Pictures

These are usually chosen to blend with or compliment the theme and colour of the room in which they are to be displayed. Small pictures are often hung in groups on one wall. The choice of frame should be appropriate in style to both the room and the picture.

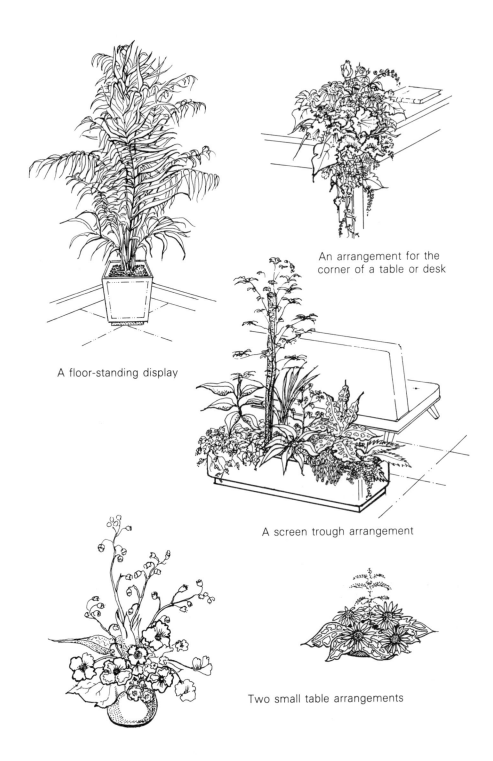

An arrangement for the
corner of a table or desk

A floor-standing display

A screen trough arrangement

Two small table arrangements

15

Sculptures

Large, older buildings may be suitable for a limited number of sculptures. Many modern buildings use ornamental items made in either traditional or futuristic style. Care needs to be taken when planning to incorporate these into the design for a room.

Photographs and Maps

Large areas of wall may be successfully covered by a reproduction of an enlarged antique photograph, or by a map of a local area or beauty spot. This may increase customer interest in the premises and can be a very effective form of interior decoration.

Glass Cabinets

These may form a room-divider, or panels that provide extra light and a valuable display area for items of interest or goods that may be purchased. These cabinets may be an extra source of income if they are leased to local craftsmen and traders selling jewellery or leather goods, or local craft items.

Illumination

Artificial lights should be chosen only after a thorough analysis of the effect to be created in any given section of a room, and of the light level desired. Spotlights, dimmer switches and wall-lights are all useful ways of ensuring versatility of light level and effect within the same room area. Spotlights or strip-lights are often very effective ways of lighting rooms that have any of the items previously mentioned; glass cabinets need interior lighting, and pictures must be illuminated without glare or shine.

Spotlights

Lighting

Lighting can make a sizeable contribution to the atmosphere and comfort of a room, but the safety of the room must always be considered.

Lounge areas	Flexible lighting is necessary for the varying types of activity that may be planned for these rooms – reading, writing, watching television, small meetings and receptions.
Reception area	Maximum visibility for front-office staff and hall porters is necessary, but at the same time the foyer needs to be restful, quiet and welcoming.
Restaurant and bars	General illumination is necessary for all preparation times and for breakfast service. More intimate background lighting is used for midday and evening meals. Wall-lights or spotlights are often used to create this effect.
Kitchen	Maximum visibility is essential. Fluorescent lighting is most suitable, as this will eliminate any shadows.
Bedrooms	Background lighting can be decorative, supplemented by lighting at certain key points; for example, bracket or table lamps at the bed-side, and filament or strip-lights above mirrors to give the most direct light.
Stairways and hallways	These must be lit so that there are no shadows in unexpected places. Lighting from the ceiling will emphasise the edge and tread of each step. Two-way switching on staircases is essential. In all hours of darkness the staircases should be lit to ensure safety.

Colours

Factors to be considered when planning the colour scheme for an area or room which is to be used by members of the general public include the following:

Atmosphere	The image and type of establishment, and therefore the type and age of the customers likely to be using the area.
Colours	Existing colours which have to be considered – any new colours should either complement or blend with the existing scheme.
Size	Some colours make a room look larger than it really is – plain, light colours for example, whereas dark colours tend to make a room seem smaller.
Patterns	Designs need to be very carefully chosen – large patterns and stripes may be used in very large, open areas, but smaller, fine designs can be used in most areas. These may either blend into the general colour scheme or stand out more as they catch the direct light.

The colour wheel

To create successful colour schemes, it is necessary to understand colour combinations – for which the 'colour wheel' is useful.

The following points should be remembered:

- Red, blue and yellow are the three primary colours.
- Secondary colours are made by mixing two primary colours in equal proportions.
- Mixing a primary and secondary colour gives a tertiary colour.

Successful colour combinations can be created by following these colour scheme rules:

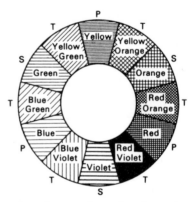

Colour wheel: P – primary colour, S – secondary colour (two primary colours mixed), T – tertiary colour (primary plus secondary colours mixed)

- *Triad colour scheme* – three primary, secondary or tertiary colours are used together; one colour should be strong and the other two soft or muted.
- *Complementary colour scheme* – contrasting pairs of colours are used, exactly opposite each other on the wheel; a bright tone should be used for a small area, with a muted tone for the rest.
- *Split complementary colour scheme* – a particular colour is used with the two on either side of its contrast.
- *Analogous colour scheme* – related colours (side by side on the wheel) are used. A contrast colour opposite one of the group may be used as an accent colour.

Assessment activities

1(a) Find out about and describe the method used by the Automobile Association to grade hotels in the United Kingdom.
 (b) Discuss the purpose of this grading system.

2(a) Draw a plan of a hotel games room/children's room.
 (b) Describe the items that you consider should be included in this room.
 (c) Indicate the advantages and disadvantages of this type of provision for young persons in hotels.

3 Design a brochure for a hotel weekend-break promotion.

4(a) Draw a plan to scale for a student bedroom which could be found in a university hall of residence.
 (b) Describe the colours, furnishings and fittings that you have included.

5(a) Arrange a visit to your local hospital, taking particular note of the furnishings and fittings in a patients' ward.
 (b) Describe the patients' ward, including details of the types of furnishing used.

Unit 2:

Cleaning Systems

The purpose of cleaning

Cleaning removes as much dust, dirt, grease, bacteria and debris as possible, given the limitations of staff and the length of time available.

The reasons for cleaning are as follows:

- To maintain a safe and clean environment.
- To preserve furniture and fittings in good condition.
- To maintain an attractive environment in which to live and work.

The methods used will depend upon the following:

- The type of soiling.
- The material or surface to be cleaned.
- The standard of cleanliness required.

General principles of cleaning

- To remove loose dust and dirt.
- To choose the simplest method first, using the least harmful cleaning agent.
- The surface should be restored to its original state at the end of the process.
- The dust and dirt should be removed and collected in such a way that it cannot cause harm to any additional surface.
- The process should use the minimum possible equipment, cleaning agents and time.

Dust, dirt and debris

Dust consists of organic and inorganic substances. Generally, dust is termed as dirt when it becomes trapped in moisture or grease; as a result it causes further dust to accumulate.

Inorganic substances
- Grit
- Soot
- Dry earth
- Fragments from pavements

- Sand
- Chalk

Organic substances
- Vegetable life – leaves, pollen, grass
- Animal life – hair, skin, fur, droppings
- Bacteria
- Yeast and moulds

It may be taken into buildings on people's feet, blown in or generated on-site.

By foot
- Silica
- Subsoil
- Leaves

Air-borne
- Dust
- Pollen
- Coal-dust

Generated on site
- Hair and skin
- Fluff
- Food crumbs

- Chewing-gum paper
- Plant seeds
- Feathers
- Ash
- Paper

The prevention of dirt accumulation

Dirt can be prevented from going beyond the entrance to a building by the use of antistatic dust-control mats. These may also be fitted as complete carpeted areas in hotel foyers and in shops, offices and other commercial premises. Dust-control mats must be:

- safe, non-slip and lie flat upon the floor surface;
- large enough to take a minimum of two complete strides;
- absorbent and easy to keep clean.

Doormats and scrapers may also be used to remove most of the debris from feet, before actually entering the building. These are often located in porch areas and may be fitted into a well in the floor surface – to catch the dust and prevent any movement of the mat. They may be made of:

- coconut fibres;
- rubber-webbed link;
- synthetic impregnated material.

To prevent dirt and soiling:

Area	Outside	Door/entrance	Hall/foyer
	1 Keep area well swept. 2 Keep free from litter, leaves, grit, snow, water.	1 Build a porch. 2 Fit a canopy. 3 Use a scraper mat. 4 Use exterior mat. 5 Double entrance doors, with a dust-control mat between the two doors.	1 Fit dust-control carpeting in entire area. 2 Provide waste-paper bins. 3 Provide ashtrays. 4 Provide umbrella stand.
Method	1 Include area on regular cleaning schedule. 2 Remove snow, ice and laves. 3 Keep level and well drained to remove rain water.	1 Regular cleaning of mats and porch area. 2 Design porch to reduce draughts.	1 Fit a circular door to eliminate draughts. 2 Include in a frequent cleaning programme, for example day and night cleaning.

Cleaning organisation

A daily routine is maintained to ensure that:

- the whole establishment is cleaned regularly;
- the work is evenly allocated between the staff;
- the housekeeper and staff know who is responsible for any given area;
- the work can be completed in the time allocated;
- each member of staff has a daily work-schedule;
- the staff are provided with adequate equipment and cleaning agents to enable them to complete their work to the required standard;
- the housekeeper can run her department within the departmental budget.

Frequency of cleaning

Some cleaning has to be completed daily, some weekly, and some will only be required at less frequent intervals; this may be monthly, quarterly or even yearly, depending on the standards of the establishment and the degree of soiling. Whatever the schedule, all staff must be trained to remove stains and marks as they occur, so that they do not become ingrained and permanent.

Daily cleaning (dust removal)	Weekly cleaning (wet cleaning)	Special cleaning (extra cleaning)
1 Dry dusting. 2 Damp dusting. 3 Dust removal/suction. 4 Dust control/ mopping.	1 Wipe paintwork. 2 Wash floors, windows. 3 Wax woodwork, furniture. 4 High dust control. (In addition to daily clean.)	Complete rooms are stripped and thoroughly cleaned. This may require extra staff and the use of outside contractors.
Completed daily in all areas and rooms.	Completed once a week. It may be incorporated into the daily routine by cleaning a different item each day.	Completed as staffing and conditions allow, and when rooms are vacant and in need of extra attention. Records are kept of each room cleaned in this way.

Block cleaning

This is a method of cleaning used in halls of residence, when all rooms are vacant at the same time and are situated close together. These rooms are occupied by the same residents for the entire year and are fitted with lockable cupboards for valuables. Sets of rooms are cleaned in sequence instead of the normal method, where each room is individually opened and cleaned. It is a quicker method and ensures that all tasks are completed in each room.

Cleaning and preparing rooms

Aim – to create an acceptable level of cleanliness and a pleasant, tidy room.

Procedure

1 VISUAL	• Check the level of dust. • Identify any stains or damage. • Check heat and humidity level.
2 REMOVE	• Litter, old newspapers, dead flowers. • Used crokery, glassware, trays and ashtrays. • Additional furniture that is no longer required.
3 PREPARE	• Equipment necessary to clean the room. • Cleaning agents required to clean the room. • Check any clean linen required for the room.
4 COLLECT	• Clean ashtrays. • Fresh flowers/plants. • Give-away products, notepaper, menu cards, newspapers.
5 ACTION	• Walls – dry/damp dust as necessary, cleaning above eye-level first. • Furniture – dry/damp dust or polish as necessary, check handles, knobs and castors. • Floor – clear small objects, suction clean/dry dust removal; wet clean if appropriate.
6 CHECK	• Arrange furniture. • Position flowers, ashtrays, give-away products, newspapers, linen. • Balance ventilation and heating. • Leave room ready for use.
7 REPLACE	• All cleaning equipment must be cleaned and put away ready for use another day. • Used linen is sent to linen-room to be laundered.

General points
• Leave the room in the condition that you would like to find it.
• Always check that all cleaning agents and equipment are removed.

- Ensure that the room is locked if necessary after cleaning.
- Check the lights and other electrical items; leave ready for use.
- Adjust the curtains and blinds according to the time of day.
- Report to the supervisor any damage or breakages which are found while cleaning the room.
- Use safety warning notices if the wet floor cleaning process is to be used.

The housekeeping service room

This is a room in an area of the hotel near the bedrooms serviced by room-maids. They work from this service room and keep all their equipment in it. It is used in establishments where early-morning tea is served in the bedrooms, and where housemaids' trolleys are not used.

Functions of the service room

- To ensure the tidy appearance of the residential areas.
- To enable the housekeeping staff to work in an organised manner.
- To enable room servicing to be prompt and efficient.

Equipment in the service room may include the following:

- Early-morning tea-tray
  - trays, crockery, cutlery;
  - tea, coffee, milk, sugar, biscuits.
- Room-servicing items
  - manual cleaning equipment;
  - electrical cleaning equipment;
  - cleaning agents.
- Fittings
  - instant boiling-water unit or electric kettle;
  - electric toaster, refrigerator;
  - clock, internal telephone.
- Equipment for guests
  - spare beds and bedding;
  - hot-water bottles, electric blankets;
  - hair-driers, razors, irons.

1 Refuse container/shute.
2 Cupboards/shelves.
3 Stainless-steel sink.
4 Work-top, socket.
5 Refrigerator.
6 Work-top, with shelves below for trays.
7 Housekeeping equipment store area.

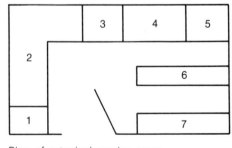

Plan of a typical service room

Specific areas and cleaning problems

Area	Features	Likely problems
Halls, foyers	Dust-control matting/ carpet. Heavy-duty floor covering. Light, welcoming atmosphere.	People constantly walking through with luggage. Leads directly outside, causing draughts and litter.
Stairs, corridors	Heavy-duty floor covering. Quiet and non-slip. Stain-resistant. Curved corners.	Large number of people constantly walking about. Crevices on stair-rises and sides will harbour dust.
Passenger lifts	Dust-control floor covering. Kick-guards and hand-rail/ bar around the walls.	In constant use. A small, confined space to clean. Needs to be aired regularly. Damp-clean walls daily.
Offices, reception areas	Desks, chairs and shelves. Hard-wearing floor coverings. Well lit and ventilated. Venetian blinds or curtains. Plants.	Files and documents must not be moved. Telephones need to be cleaned and disinfected. Keyboards and VDU need antistatic dusting. Waste or shredded paper. Security area.
Computer rooms	Atmosphere and temperature is constantly controlled. Dust-free fittings, and floor is sealed.	Double-filter specialist suction cleaner. Special training and supervision of staff. High security area.
Lounges, common rooms	Comfortable, extensive upholstered seating. Television. Coffee tables. Periodicals. Plants. Ashtrays.	Needs to be well ventilated when being cleaned because of ashtrays, newspapers and litter. Seating will need regular suction cleaning/damp dusting.
Kitchens, cellars	Impervious surfaces for walls, ceilings, floors, work-surfaces. Equipment permanently fixed in position. Standards set by the Food Hygiene Regulations.	Restricted floor areas under and around equipment. Heavy soiling and grease to be cleaned away. Floor gullies and drains. Special staff training/supervision. Security area.

Area	Features	Likely problems
Bars, restaurants	Impervious surfaces for floors, walls and shelves. Equipment fixed and some small in size. Carpets and seating in public areas. Standards set by the Food Hygiene Regulations.	Food particles and beverage stains. Litter, bottle tops and empty crates and bottles. Beer pipes and pumps, cooling equipment. Will need to be well ventilated. Should look clean and inviting – no odour of cleaning agents or food.

Hospital cleanliness

Effective organisation is an essential element of hospital cleanliness. An infection control committee works with the domestic services staff to give advice on infection control.

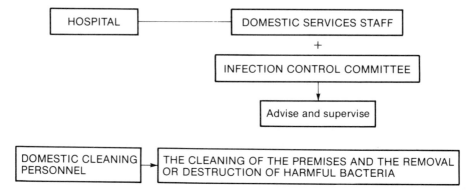

Successful infection control depends upon the following:

- inter-departmental co-operation,
- adequate training procedures,
- efficient supervisory staff,
- adequate selection and care of equipment,
- correct selection and use of cleaning agents.

Staff
- Training and awareness of contamination dangers and cross-infection.
- Induction training and retraining schemes.
- High standards of personal hygiene.
- Adequate protective clothing and procedures for laundering and replacing.
- Adequate daily staff supervision.

28

- Pride in their role within the workforce, and its importance.
- A consistent, methodical manner of work.

Agents/equipment
- Sachets of liquid agents to ensure correct dilution.
- Buckets with capacity markings to ensure correct dilution.
- Sufficient supply of agents and equipment to ensure an acceptable standard of work is maintained.
- Adequate maintenance of equipment to ensure its efficient operation.
- Adequate autoclave and pasteurising facilities for equipment.
- Sufficient storage areas for sterilised equipment.
- Adequate areas for the washing, emptying and daily maintenance of cleaning equipment.

Cleaning equipment in hospitals

Electrical equipment

Suction cleaners
- Always choose models with a double filter for the dust.
- Should be fitted with disposable dust bags, which may be incinerated after use.
- Always check the noise level when the machine is switched on and moved along the floor.
- Check that the air flow/outlet does not create too much air movement in the surrounding area.
- Ensure that there is high suction power even for light dust particles.

Buffing/polishing machines
- Check the noise level when carrying out each process.
- Select a model that will remove dust and buff/polish in one action.
- Ensure that the head of the machine can reach into corners and under fittings.

Wet floor-cleaning machines
- Select a model which will scrub and remove slurry in one action to ensure the fastest possible floor cleaning.
- Check the level of noise when the machine is in use.
- Choose a model with a head that will reach into the corners of the floor, and under equipment/fittings.
- Ensure that the machine will leave the surface of the floor free from moisture.
- All removable parts must be of a material that will enable them to be sterilised (brushes, tanks, hose).

Manual equipment

Trolleys – these must be easily cleaned, have rounded corners and be quiet to move around. The castors should be large and well protected.

Buckets – these should have capacity markings on the side and must be of material that can be sterilised. Handles, wringers and castors should be easily cleaned.

Cloths and mops – these must be made of material that may be sterilised, or be disposable. The handles/heads should not become chipped, as this can harbour bacteria.

Brooms/dustpans – these should be of a material that will enable them to be sterilised. They should be rounded at the edges and free from grooves or dents.

Chutes – for linen or rubbish. They should be made of impervious material, have easily cleaned doors/flaps, and efficient emptying, bailing and cleaning procedures. They may harbour bacteria if not cleaned properly.

Cross-infection in hospitals

Cross-infection may be caused by staff inadvertently passing bacteria from one area to another by using contaminated equipment on more than one surface. With efficient training and supervision, this should not occur.

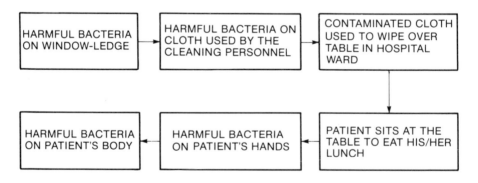

From this one example it is easy to appreciate the importance of adequate care and strict working methods in hospitals.

Safety of hospital premises and fittings

The following aspects should be regularly checked for safety. Any faults should be reported for maintenance immediately.

Floors

- These should be non-slip, with rounded corners to the skirting board.
- The surface should be impervious and quiet to the touch.

Surfaces

- These should be impervious, with no cracks or chips to the outer surface.
- The finish should be smooth and a light colour to show up any dirt.

Doorways

- These should be wide, with the ability to swing in either direction.
- Vision windows should be fitted to all doors.

Corridors

- These should be kept free from miscellaneous items of equipment/fittings.
- Emergency exits should be clearly marked and not obstructed.
- All hand-rails and ramps should be secure and clean.

Electricity

- An adequate number of wall sockets should be available, to eliminate flexes trailing along the floors.
- Regular safety checks should be made on patients' head phones.

Furnishings

- Sealed tubular framework on all beds, stretchers and trolleys will be easier to keep free from bacteria.
- All curtains, blinds and screens should be washable.
- Impervious covers should be fitted to all upholstery items.

Mobility aids

- These should be easily cleaned, with strong wheels.
- Tyres, rubber stops and brakes should be checked regularly.
- Walking aids and crutches should be checked regularly and kept as clean as possible.

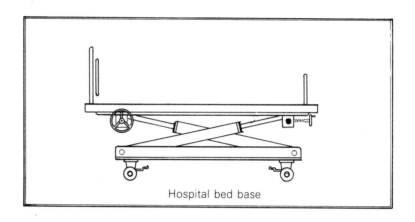

Hospital bed base

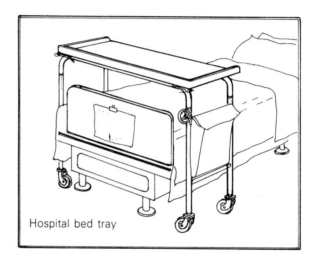

Hospital bed tray

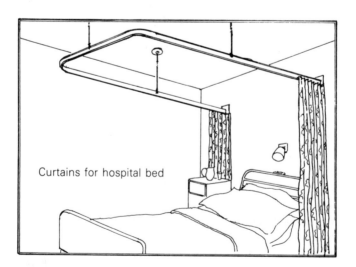

Curtains for hospital bed

Wall

Floor Covering

Floor

Sealed skirting

Waste

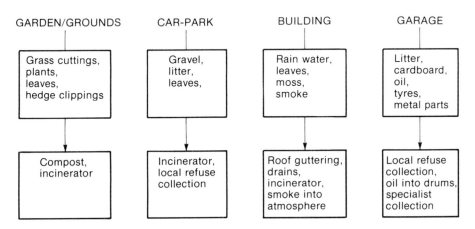

GARDEN/GROUNDS	CAR-PARK	BUILDING	GARAGE
Grass cuttings, plants, leaves, hedge clippings	Gravel, litter, leaves,	Rain water, leaves, moss, smoke	Litter, cardboard, oil, tyres, metal parts
Compost, incinerator	Incinerator, local refuse collection	Roof guttering, drains, incinerator, smoke into atmosphere	Local refuse collection, oil into drums, specialist collection

External origins of waste

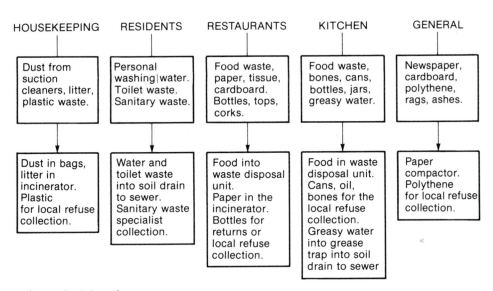

HOUSEKEEPING	RESIDENTS	RESTAURANTS	KITCHEN	GENERAL
Dust from suction cleaners, litter, plastic waste.	Personal washing\water. Toilet waste. Sanitary waste.	Food waste, paper, tissue, cardboard. Bottles, tops, corks.	Food waste, bones, cans, bottles, jars, greasy water.	Newspaper, cardboard, polythene, rags, ashes.
Dust in bags, litter in incinerator. Plastic for local refuse collection.	Water and toilet waste into soil drain to sewer. Sanitary waste specialist collection.	Food into waste disposal unit. Paper in the incinerator. Bottles for returns or local refuse collection.	Food in waste disposal unit. Cans, oil, bones for the local refuse collection. Greasy water into grease trap into soil drain to sewer	Paper compactor. Polythene for local refuse collection.

Internal origins of waste

Items of waste which cause problems include the following:

Foods

- Beef bones, because of their size.
- Fish bones and skins, because they are slippery.
- Onion skins, because they are tough.
- Chicken skins, because they are tough and slippery.

General

- Polythene and plastic, because these do not disintegrate.
- Oil because it must always be poured into cans and sealed for disposal.
- Glass items may be recycled if collected separately.
- Metal, if not to be recycled, must be compressed as much as possible to reduce its bulk.
- Rubber tyres from garages are usually recycled and collected separately. They are difficult to stack and keep tidy.

Hospitals

- Clinical and surgical waste must be incinerated.
- Sharp syringes and scalpels need specialist disposal.

Offices

- Security papers and documents are shredded, then placed in an incinerator.
- Waste paper and cardboard is compacted, baled and collected for recycling.

Dangers of inadequate waste disposal

- Cross-infection caused.
- Spread of contamination is likely.
- Breeding grounds for bacteria are made.
- Flies and rodents are attracted.
- Insect infestation may result.
- Foul odours arise.
- Untidy appearance.
- Standards of hygiene lapse.
- Staff become sloppy.
- Cats and dogs are attracted.
- Empties that have a deposit value are lost.
- A bad impression is created.
- Risk of fine under the Food Hygiene Regulations.

Refuse areas – dustbins

- Bins must be lined with an internal sack, and should be emptied after each work shift.
- Interior bins should be as clean as all other items in a room.
- Exterior bins should be kept in a covered area that is clean and tidy.
- Animals should be prevented from access to the bin area.
- Bins must be kept cool, clean and dry, each with a well-fitting lid.
- The bins must be cleaned regularly.
- The handles and lids of the bins need to be very clean

to prevent any risk of cross-infection.
- There should be a regular collection service arranged for the bins to be emptied.
- After emptying, bins should all be cleaned with a high-pressure water cleaner and bleach.

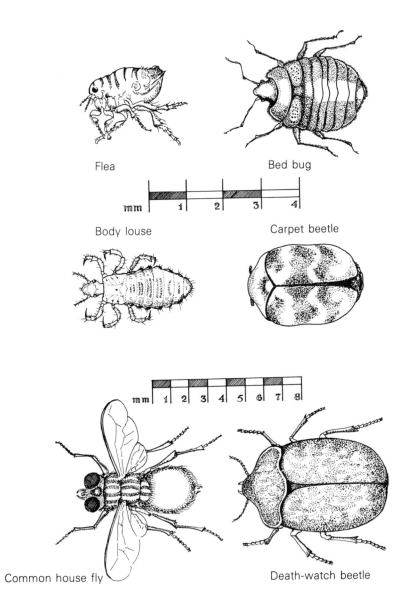

Flea

Bed bug

Body louse

Carpet beetle

Common house fly

Death-watch beetle

Pest control

Any of the following types of pest may be found in residential buildings. They should be eliminated as soon as they are seen, and the local authority environmental health officer should be called in to advise and assist if necessary.

Type	Size/colour	Area found	Infestation signs	Treatment
Lice	2 mm, grey/ brown.	Human hair/scalp.	Sight, eggs, bites, blood.	Clean hair and scalp, maintain personal hygiene.
Fleas	2–3 mm, gingery/ brown.	Domestic pet, unclean humans.	Bites and irritation on skin.	Clean habits/premises, fumigation of the premises, no pets.
Bed bugs	0.5 cm, brown.	Unclean bedding, upholstery.	Bite on skin which causes itching.	Clean bedding and all upholstery regularly.
Carpet beetles	2 mm round, black.	Unclean wool carpets.	Holes in carpet	Suction clean regularly; shampoo occasionally.
Wasps	2 cm, black and yellow.	Food areas. Summer months	Noise, sight, spoilt foods, bites/sting.	Place screen on window, cover all foods, ultra-violet light tray.
Moths	20 mm, brown.	Warm, dark areas and fabrics, un-disturbed places, linen stores.	Eggs on fabrics, holes in curtains, bedding and upholstery.	Regular suction cleaning of fabric areas, upholstery, well-lit linen store, linen used in rotation.
Wood-boring beetles: 1 House longhorn	25 mm, black.	Soft timber in house construction.	Damaged timber, white pellets.	Pre-treat timber with preservative, call in specialist.
2 Powder-post beetle.	5 mm, brown.	Timber in yards, oak.	Wood is reduced to a powder.	Wood sprayed with insecticide, purchase from reputable yard.
3 Death-watch beetle	7–9 mm, brown with yellow patch.	Hard woods with fungal decay, churches.	Exit holes 3 mm wide, gritty pellets.	Call in an expert to cut out timbers and fumigate, then replace.

Type	Size/colour	Area found	Infestation signs	Treatment
4 Weevils	3–5 mm, brown, long snouts.	Timber with wet rot.	Wood splits with the grain, exit holes 1–2 mm.	Prevention of wet rot – consult an expert.
Rats	24 cm body, brown/black.	Lift shafts, dustbins.	Droppings. Gnawing marks, sight.	Clean, tidy premises – no dirty areas to attract a rat.
Mice	9 cm, grey/brown.	Dark cupboards, lofts, under floorboards.	Droppings, noise, gnawing marks, sight.	Clean premises, well lit, buildings in good repair, rotate stock.
House flies	8 mm long, black.	Dustbins, open food.	Sight, noise.	Clean bins daily, well ventilated premises.

Dry rot

Wet rot

Dry rot

This is the name given to the decay of timber caused by dampness. A fungi plant is found growing on the damp timber area.

The cause of damp could be any of the following, and needs to be investigated at once by an expert:

Wet rot

Here the fungus attacks the timber used in the building construction and spreads over the wall. It is commonly found in cellars and in window and door frames which have not been treated with a wood preservative. It is also found on outdoor fences and

37

- Rising damp – no damp-proof course.
- Broken exterior pipes.
- Poor roof drainage.
- Blocked guttering.
- Soil banked up against side of premises.

gates. An expert should be called in to deal with any outbreak before it has time to spread.

The following chart gives a summary of temperatures for the purposes of housekeeping.

Approximate temperature (^{o}C)	Housekeeping	Theory	Bacteria
180	Sterilisation oven, dry heat.		
120	Sterilisation heat, autoclave.		
100		Water boiling point.	Bacteria killed.
90	Very hot wash – linen, cotton.		
80		Crockery sterilising water.	
70	Wash soiled linen and equipment.		
60	Hot wash polyester.	Yeast killed.	
55			Maximum bacteria growth.
50	Hand-hot wash.		
40	Medium wash, wool, coloureds.		
30	Cool wash, silk.	Yeast growth.	Rapid bacteria growth.
20	Indoor comfort level.		
15	Bedroom comfort level.		
10			Minimum bacteria growth.
5		Refrigerator temperature.	Bacteria cease to multiply –
0		Water freezes.	dormant.

Bacteria need the following conditions to grow/multiply:	For the prevention of bacterial growth:
• food and time,	• clean the area thoroughly and regularly,
• oxygen,	• filter all incoming air, reduce overcrowding, encourage fresh air and sunshine,
• water,	• adjust humidity of building, reduce condensation level,
• heat.	• sterilise equipment and linen at $100°C$.

Washrooms and bathrooms

Wherever or whatever the type, style and size of the washroom, the basic principles relating to the cleanliness of the fitments and fittings are the same. The following points should always be remembered:

- Washrooms are used by members of the public/workforce/guests, and in all cases present a potential health hazard.
- Cross-infection risks are high, as there are many shared surfaces in any bath/washroom.
- Dirty/soiled rooms are unpleasant to use – this will cause a further layer of dirt.
- Soiled/dirty/uncared for wash/bathrooms will reflect a poor and unpleasant image to the general public.
- Uncared for washrooms will have the effect of reducing the standards of cleanliness elsewhere in the premises.
- This reduction in standards of cleanliness will have an adverse effect upon future trading.

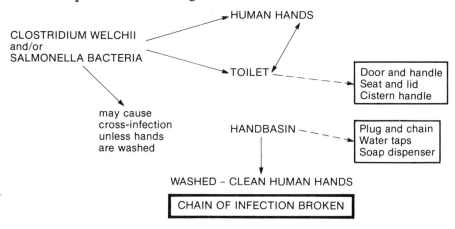

Toilets should be kept:
Clean – to minimise bacterial growth.
Tidy – to encourage cleanliness.
Airy – to minimise odours and bacterial growth.
Hygienic – to ensure standards are maintained.

Toilets should be supplied with:
• hot and cold water for hand washing,
• a nail brush to encourage clean hands and nails,
• soap to ensure that bacteria are destroyed when hands are washed.
• hand-drying facilities which do not harbour bacteria,
• toilet paper in a germ-free container.

Fitments should include waste bins, 'now wash your hands' notices, and sanitary bins in female toilets.

Cleaning toilets, washrooms and bathrooms

Stage	Action	Reason
1 Ventilate	Open all windows or activate extractor fans.	To eliminate unpleasant odours, and to reduce the number of air-borne, harmful bacteria.
2 Litter	Prop open doors. Put a 'cleaning in progress' sign on outer door. Sweep floor. Remove refuse and litter.	Litter, refuse and dust will harbour bacteria and insects and cause unpleasant odours and infection.
3(a) Water-closet	Flush, then brush inside vigorously. Apply acid toilet cleanser.	To remove traces of paper and debris, organic stains and lime-scale stains.
3(b) Urinals	Flush, then stop automatic flush mechanism while the walls and base trough are scrubbed thoroughly. Apply acid cleanser.	To remove traces of urine and dust, which harbour bacteria and cause unpleasant odours.

Stage	Action	Reason
3(c) External surfaces	Wash all exterior surfaces of the WC urinals and basins. Use hot water and germicidal detergent.	To remove smears, urine traces, dust, harmful bacteria. Cross-infection may occur from contact with seat, handles and taps.
4 Hand-basins, drinking fountains	Wash thoroughly, using non-scratch cleanser. Pay attention to taps, plugs, chains, splashbacks, soap dispensers, and water outlet on drinking fountains.	These can cause cross-infection, as the hands are in direct contact with the basin. To remove harmful bacteria, debris, scum marks, soap.
5 Sundries	Replenish soap dispensers, towels, toilet paper, contents of slot machines, litter containers. Adjust ventilation and doors.	To ensure an adequate supply for the staff/guests/general public.
6 Surfaces	Damp dust window-ledges, doors, other surfaces. Use germicidal detergent solution in spray.	To remove dust, finger marks and harmful bacteria.
7 WC and urinal	Turn on flushing mechanism for urinals. Flush WC. Polish up all seats, lids, cisterns, handles.	To spread the acid cleanser evenly around surfaces.
8 Floor	Clean floor in appropriate manner.	Removal of dust and bacteria.
9 Final check	Check. Remove cleaning notice.	Ensure room is ready for use.

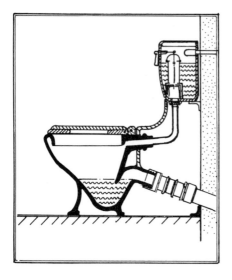

Sectional view of water-closet
(with low-level cistern)

Sectional view of bidet

(*Note* U bends prevent odours
entering room from waste
pipes)

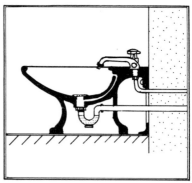

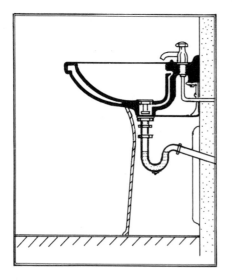

Sectional view of wash-basin
(with pedestal base)

Surfaces and finishes likely to be used in washrooms

Item	Material	Areas	Characteristics
Water-closets, urinals, hand-basins	Enameled steel	Residential and public areas/rooms.	Hardwearing, but will chip and scratch.
	Porcelain	Luxury bathrooms.	Not very strong — for light usage only.
	Stainless steel	Public washrooms, industrial washrooms, work areas.	Very strong and will stay good looking even with very hard use.
Walls	Painted or sealed brickwork or a smooth concrete	Public and in-dustrial washrooms, work areas.	Needs regular maintenance. Graffiti proof seal or paint should be used.
	Ceramic tiles	Industrial and residential areas, catering areas.	Easily cleaned and impervious.
	Vinyl wallpaper	Luxury residential areas.	Short life, will tear and peel with wear.
Floors	Sealed concrete	Industrial and public areas.	Uneven surface that will need regular resealing.
	Quarry tiles	Industrial and public areas, catering areas.	An impervious surface, easily cleaned, very strong and hardwearing.
	Ceramic tiles	Residential areas.	Attractive, impervious strong surface, easily cleaned.
	Sealed ther-moplastic tiles/sheet.	Residential and interior public areas.	Need to be sealed regularly. Not able to withstand constant dampness.

Assessment activities

1(a) Look around the building at your place of work or training and list the organic and inorganic particles of dust and debris that you find.
 (b) Find out where these substances have come from and how they entered the premises.

2(a) Find out how your classroom or place of work is cleaned, and by which methods.
 (b) Discuss whether the standard of cleanliness is adequate for the room's purpose.

3 Identify and describe the specific cleaning problems in your place of work. List the reasons for these problems.

4 Find out how the various types of waste items and refuse are disposed of at your place of work or training.

5 Describe the differences that you will expect to find between the fittings and surfaces in a luxury hotel bathroom and a bathroom in a boarding school.

Unit 3:

Cleaning Agents and Linen Care

Cleaning agents

General supervisory

- Supplier – use the minimum number of cleaning agents and suppliers.
- Dispensing – issue to staff in conveniently sized units/bottles.
- Training – adequate staff training to ensure no misuse of cleaning agents.
- Supervision – regular staff supervision to ensure the correct dilution of cleaning agents.
- Safety – ensure that staff adhere to all aspects of the HASAWA.
- Checking – of all cleaning standards, and of cost efficiency of issue of cleaning agents.

Selection of cleaning agents

Consideration must be given to the following:
- The types of material and surface to be cleaned.
- The types of equipment to be used.
- The capabilities of the staff.
- The cleaning agent unit size and type of container (bulk/aerosol/litre/sachets/spray refills).
- The availability of agents and reordering procedures.
- The minimum order, costs, and delivery.
- Compatability of various cleaning agents used.
- The time required to use the agents effectively versus the time available.

Storing cleaning agents

- The store-room must be convenient for deliveries, and locked when not in use.
- It must be well ventilated, well lit and free from dampness.
- There should be adequate shelving for the cleaning agents.
- There needs to be adequate issuing facilities and space for staff to work.
- There must be a storekeeper's desk for the recording of stock cards/sheets.
- There needs to be a methodical, reliable storekeeper employed.
- Stock must be rotated, with the oldest items issued first.
- The agents must be stored in a safe way – no inflammable items near heat.
- There should be regular issuing times and procedures.
- There needs to be thorough recording and reordering procedures.

Definitions of cleaning agents

Type	Area of use	Safety	Method of use
DETERGENTS			
Liquid	Cleansing food-preparation items.	Clean sink nozzle regularly.	Sink dispensers; rinse and sterilise items after wash.
With a Steriliser	Cleansing food-preparation items.	Pre-wash is essential.	Dishwashing machine, rinse well, dry in racks.
Low-foam powder	Automatic machines. Textile washing.	Measured amount per machine load.	Automatic or manual feed of detergent.
Powder	Manual textile washing.	Measured quantity, rinse well.	Rotary or twin-tub machines. Hand washing.
Enzyme powder	Removal of protein stains from textiles.	Pre-wash/soak, rinse well.	Soak or use as a washing agent.
Mild alkali	Removal of water-based polish.	Check dilution, rinse well.	Mop or machine application. Removal of floor polishes.
Strong alkali	De-greasing of kitchen equipment and fittings.	Wear protective clothing, rinse well, ventilate area well.	Soak for a limited time. Scrape off well. Wash items well with hot water. Dry.
With a bactericide	Where extra cleanliness is re-quired, e.g. hospitals.	Measured amount in sachets, per litre of water.	Damp dusting. Mopping. Floor scrubbing.
Solvent based	For removal of sol-vent based polishes.	*Not* on PVC or thermoplastic.	Mop or machine ap-plication, rinse well.
Neutral cleanser	General cleaning, and sealed floors of PVC and thermoplastic.	Dilute 1:60/80. For floors, dilute 1:40.	Spray/damp dusting. Damp mop, spray buff or scrub-bing the floors.
Acid	De-scaling, and the removal of calcium salts and stains.	Wear protective clothing. Rinse. Limited soaking.	Water-closet pans and urinal, bains-marie. Water boilers.

Type	Area of use	Safety	Method of use
Carpet cleaning	Carpets and carpet tiles.	Check dilution per litre of water.	Machine application; when dry suction clean.

SOAPS

Type	Area of use	Safety	Method of use
Block	General cleaning.	Use sparingly; rinse well.	Scrubbing untreated wooden surfaces, shelves.
Flakes	Washing natural textiles.	Dissolve prior to use; rinse.	For delicate natural textiles. Hand washing.
Powder	Textiles.	Dissolve prior to use; rinse.	Machine or hand washing of textiles.
Toilet	Personal hygiene.	Small blocks to prevent wastage.	Personal washing of the body. Keep well drained.
Liquid	Personal hygiene.	Clean nozzle to prevent clogging. Clean dispenser.	Soap dispenser fixed to wall in public toilets.

GENERAL

Type	Area of use	Safety	Method of use
Soda – sodium carbonate	Degreasing drains and floor gullies. Polivit silver cleaning.	Never use with aluminium pans. Rinse well.	Use very hot water to dissolve the soda before use.
Bleach – sodium hypo-chloride	Kills bacteria in drains. Removes stains. Cleans dustbins.	*Poisonous* – use with great care.	Use protective gloves. Short soak only; rinse well. Dilute 1:40.
Ammonia	Grease emulsifier. Windows and glass.	Use with care. Dilute 1:40.	Solution sprayed on to window, then buffed with soft cloth.
Distilled vinegar	Removal of mild water stains from baths. Diluted solution for cleaning wooden furniture.	Use diluted 1:20–1:40.	Solution rubbed over with a soft cloth; rinse well, dry immediately.

Type	Area of use	Safety	Method of use
ABRASIVES			
Non-scratch cream/powder	Ceramics, plastics, stainless steel, enamel items.	Use sparingly; rinse well.	Apply with a damp cloth; rinse immediately. May scratch with over use.
Paste	Ceramic enamel.	Rinse well.	Apply sparingly, and dry the cleaned surface.
Powder	Aluminium, terrazzo, quarry tiles.	Rinse well.	Use sparingly; rinse well.
POLISH – spirit/solvent based wax			
Paste	Wooden floors.	Non-slip type; rub off well.	Apply thinly, buff when dry. Apply in sections across the floor.
Liquid	Wooden floors.	Warm before applying to ensure the wax and solvents are mixed.	Apply sparingly with a mop, applicator or spray unit. Buff up well.
POLISH – water-based synthetic emulsion			
Dry bright	Vinyl, thermoplastic rubber, terrazzo, resin floors.	Must be an anti-slip variety.	Dries after application in 20 minutes. Easy to apply, dries with a shine.
Semi-buffable	As above for light traffic areas.	Resistant to dirt, stains and water.	Daily mopping/buffing will keep it in good condition.
Buffable	As above in heavy traffic areas.	Anti-slip. May be used where sprit-based polish is unsafe to use.	Daily dust removal and buffing to keep in good condition. Spray buff if necessary.

Type	Area of use	Safety	Method of use
Paste	Wooden unsealed surfaces.	Rub well into wood in line of grain.	Apply with a soft cloth. Buff well to produce gloss.
Cream	Unsealed carved wooded surfaces.	Apply sparingly with soft cloth.	Buff area well and remove all traces of polish between the carvings (with a brush).
Spray	Wooden areas of furniture, as 'touch-up' care.	Inflammable canister; clean spray nozzle.	Spray on to soft cloth. Use to 'touch-up' furniture. Expensive.
Teak	Use on unsealed teak wood items.	Apply sparingly.	Buff on to the surface to 'feed' the wood. Matt finish.

GENERAL PURPOSE/SYNTHETIC POLISH

Type	Area of use	Safety	Method of use
Aerosol	Vinyl, plastic, tiles, ceramics, paintwork.	Inflammable canister; clean nozzle.	Spray onto soft cloth. Use as added gloss to surfaces. Expensive.
Spray	As above	Refills available.	As above.

The pH scale and cleaning agents

From the following table it is posible to see which types of detergent and cleaning agent are acid and which are alkali. The pH scale is the method used to measure a product's acid or alkali content.

pH	Acid	pH	Mild	pH	Alkali
1		7	Soap	9	Mild alkali detergents
2	Toilet cleansers	8	Liquid detergent	10	Bleach
3	Acid detergents		Neutral detergent	11	Ammonia
4				12	Soda
5	Distilled vinegar			13	Strong alkali detergents
6				14	

Soaps

These are based on animal fats combind with caustic soda. Soap does not reduce the surface tension of the water or fat, and has poor wetting powers. It is therefore used up quickly and forms a scum, thus recontaminating the surfaces.

Synthetic detergents

These are made from agents to create a balanced mixture, which will have the following properties:

- the ability to wet soiled surfaces and to clean soiled areas;
- the ability to reduce the surface tension of fat, which forms small droplets;
- the ability to disperse the fats throughout the solution;
- the ability to soften the water, and is free rinsing.

The soiling is floated away after a successful cleansing process.

Bleach

This will whiten surfaces and kill bacteria. It is harmful to humans and should therefore never be used in a food area.

Abrasives

Scouring powder is made from pumice, detergent and sometimes bleach. The scratching properties of the powder help to remove soil deposits.

Impregnated pads of steel wool are used on aluminium pans and trays and the steel wool helps to clean the surface. The steel will go rusty if kept wet. Minimum water should be used with these pads.

Metal cleaners

These are used on unsealed decorative hard metals, such as brass, copper and silver. There are different polishes for each type of metal. It is rubbed on to the surface with a soft cloth, then buffed off.

Starch

This is used to stiffen fabrics such as cotton and linen. The fabric is washed as normal, then dipped into the solution and wrung out; it is then dried and ironed as normal.

Stain removal

Rules

- Firstly, identify the cause of the stain.
- Secondly, take appropriate action immediately.
- Thirdly, ventilate the area well.

The following table provides guidelines for the removal of stains from various surfaces.

Fabrics	Carpets
Washable – soak where possible, then wash. Non-washable – sponge area with warm water, then with diluted ammonia.	Scrape off any surplus debris with a blunt knife. Squirt with soda water from a syphon. Sponge with diluted carpet shampoo.
Wallpaper	**Furniture**
Washable – sponge lightly with warm water then use diluted neutral detergent solution. Non-washable – rub gently with a pencil eraser on the stain.	Identify the type of surface first. Blot up any liquids. Alcohol/heat marks – rub the area with metal polish, then repolish. Burn – rub with turpentine.
Remember:	**Types of stain**
Act with caution. Use mild methods first. Work from outside of stain inwards. Never smoke while using agents. Never use solvents near heat. Turn off all pilot lights. Protect skin on hands.	Absorbed – liquids which have been absorbed into the surface, such as tea and coffee. Built up – leave a surface deposit but do not penetrate the surface, e.g. nail varnish, grease. Compound – penetrate the surface and leave surface depositis, e.g. blood.

Some useful stain removers for fabrics and fibres are listed below:

- *Solvents* – acetone, methylated spirits. Dissolve grease and oil stains and lift them out of the fabric.
- *Bleaches* – sodium perborate, found in powder detergent, and hydrogen peroxide. These remove stains and are very strong.
- *Chemicals* – commercially prepared stain removers. These react chemically and remove ink rust and iron mould stains.
- *Absorbants* – Fuller's earth, french chalk, salt. These will absorb the stain from pile fabrics.
- *Enzymes* – biological synthetic detergents. Soak out protein-based stains.

General stain removal agents

- Ammonia – 1:3 dilution with water. It will neutralise acids. Test before using.
- Enzyme washing powder – soak the item first, then wash. Rinse well.
- Glycerine – use for softening staining on fabrics. Use equal parts of glycerine and warm water. Soak for a while, then wash as normal.
- Grease solvents – commercially produced stain removers for grease and oil-based stains. Read the manufacturers instructions.
- Hydrogen peroxide – a mild bleach; use 1:6 parts cold water on fabric stains.
- Borax – a mild alkali which removes acid stains on washable fabrics.
- Methylated spirit – use neat, but never on french-polished surfaces. Inflammable and poisonous. Will remove acrylic paint from fabrics.

Disinfection

The following table gives definitions of disinfection methods and uses.

Method	Definition	Use
Sterilise	The process of removing or destroying all microbial life at 100°C.	Dry heat. Hot water or steam.
Disinfect	The removal or destruction of harmful microbes (except spores) to a level not normally harmful.	Chemical Solution. Heat – 65°C for 10 minutes.
Sanitise	To disinfect and to clean, reducing the level of microbes to an acceptable level.	Chemical solution, and heat or steam. Hospitals, food and catering premises.
Antiseptic	The destruction of microbes on living tissue to a level not normally harmful to life.	Hospital use only. Medical uses.
Germicide	A chemical agent capable of killing germs usually associated with disease.	Added to soapless detergents.

Method	Definition	Use
Bactericides	A specialised chemical agent capable of killing bacteria (not spores).	Added to soapless detergents.
Bacteriostat	A chemical agent capable of inhibiting bacterial growth.	Added to soapless detergents.

Both the water and the disinfectant must be measured to produce a solution of the recommended concentration. Premeasured sachets are often used to ensure the correct dilution – one sachet per four litres of hot water. Too much disinfectant will not remove any more harmful bacteria; it will leave a smeary, sticky surface and will therefore be less effective. Disinfectants should not be used as a substitute for efficient dirt and debris removal by normal methods.

Silver

Silver may be 'solid' or 'sterling' – both are identified by their hallmark. Sterling silver usually contains a small proportion of copper, which makes it more hard wearing. Silver plate is less expensive than solid silver and signifies an inexpensive metal, such as nickel, coated with a thin layer of silver. The silver will eventually wear off this base metal and may be replated by a specialist company. Silver is easily dented if carelessly treated or dropped. When clean, silver has an attractive, shiny finish. This becomes darkened by tarnish, caused by sulphur in the atmosphere.

Sulphur + silver = silver sulphide

A smoky atmosphere contains more sulphur than clean air and causes silver to tarnish more quickly. Foods that contain sulphur, such as eggs and green, leafy vegetables, cause silver tableware and cutlery to instantly tarnish.

Cleaning silver

The aim is to remove the tarnish without damaging the silver. The following is an explanation of the *Polivit method* of tarnish removal:

Soda + aluminium produces hydrogen gas;
hydrogen gas + silver sulphide produces sulphurated hydrogen.

Thus, the tarnish is dissolved away.

54

Polivit method

The silver is washed as usual and then placed in the Polivit solution for a few seconds.

When it is removed the tarnish will have dissolved away.

The silver is then rinsed in clear, hot water, dried and buffed up ready for further use.

Restaurant silver → wash up → Polivit → rinse → dry/buff → store/re-use.

The linen-room

This is the central store where all stocks are issued and received. It should be sited near the back entrance to enable the linen to be delivered easily. But it should not be near the kitchen because linen absorbs food odours very easily. The room must be well lit and well heated. Central heating pipes around the walls will help to keep the linen aired.

Storage of linen

Linen should be stored in cupboards with well-fitting sliding doors. Each shelf should be clearly labelled to indicate its contents; linen is difficult to identify when it is folded up and neatly stacked on shelves. The linen should be issued in strict rotation, so that the entire stock receives equal wear. A counter or hatch is essential, so that the linen-room staff can have proper control of the stock, issuing clean sets of linen only upon receipt of used linen. An adequate waiting area should be provided for staff, to prevent them having to wait in the corridor.

Examples of linen-room routines

In the hotel
Each room-maid and section in the hotel has a basic stock issue of the appropriate linen. From this stock the maid supplies all the needs of the section. Room-maids normally have a stock one and a half times the amount needed to supply all their rooms. The kitchen, restaurant, bars and room-service sections all have their own supplies of clean linen.

Each day the maid receives an amount of clean linen equal to the amount of soiled linen that is handed into the linen room. Because it is essential to supply all guests with immaculately clean linen, the

55

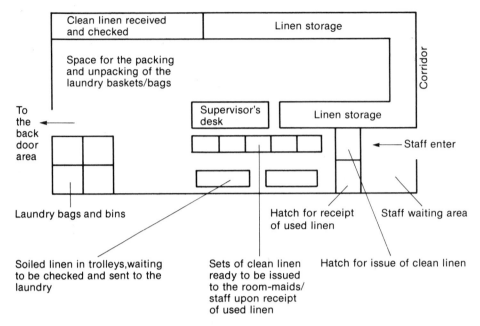

Illustration of linen-room

volume that is exchanged is normally high. The value of the linen is high in monetary terms; this means that proper checking and storage systems must be used.

In the hospital

All hospital linen is taken directly from the bed and placed into laundry bins, which contain laundry bags sewn with disposable thread. The bins are on castors for easy movement. All soiled linen is placed into one colour bag, and all fouled linen into a different colour bag. The bags are waterproof and strong; they are placed directly into the washing machine, where the thread dissolves and the linen empties out. The two categories are washed separately to prevent the risk of cross-infection.

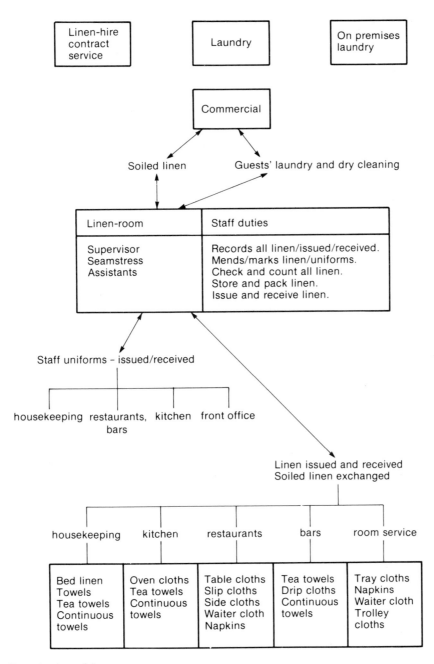

Organisation of linen

The laundry sequence in hospitals can be seen from the following diagram:

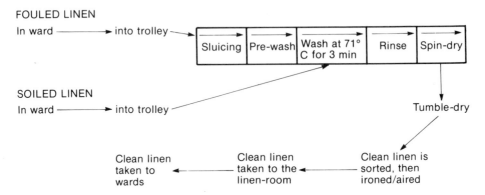

On-premise laundry

Linen may be sent to a commercial laundry to be cleaned, or there may be a laundry installed on the premises where the linen can be washed and cared for. This may be more suitable in some types of establishment, particularly in welfare, residential units, boarding schools, and units that are situated in remote parts of the country.

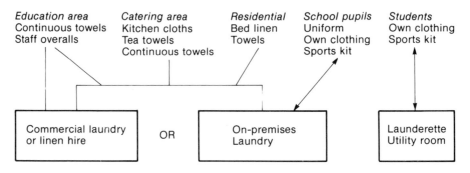

Typical laundry arrangements in boarding school/hall of residence

Linen hire

In a linen-hire scheme, linen is rented from the linen-hire company, who undertake to launder, repair and replace damaged articles. Bed linen, table linen, uniforms and towels may all be hired. The result of using this system is that it is not necessary to hold a large stock of expensive linen. Some establishments use all linen hire, while others find that a combination of hire and another system will give them the flexibility that they require (see example below).

58

Advantages of linen hire	Disadvantages of linen hire
1 Standard contract charge. 2 No money invested in stock or a depreciation account. 3 No repairs or marking to be done. 4 Linen may be monogrammed on payment of small extra charge. 5 Choice of quality and colour available.	1 Minimum charge to be paid every month. 2 May not use linen to the minimum level every month. 3 Dependent upon the hire company for the standards of linen, quality and finish. 4 No flexibility if extra items are used. 5 Delivery may be poor if weather is bad or fuel/transport strikes are called.

Dry cleaning

This is the term used for a process of cleaning fabrics with grease solvents which do not penetrate the fibres, and which enable the fibres to retain their texture, shape and colour. Dry-cleaning solvents for stain removal are benzine, carbon tetrachloride, methylated spirits, terpentine and other commercial preparations. A lot of dirt will be held in the fabric by the natural grease present; when this is removed the dirt is removed by an absorbent, such as Fuller's Earth or French Chalk. Dry-cleaning agents are useful for cleaning non-washable fabrics, but they must be used with care and caution and by experienced personnel.

Laundry equipment

Type	Fitments	Purpose	Care/maintenence
Iron — dry	—	Removing creases.	Cool, check plug/flex.
Iron — steam	Tank for water.	Pressing fabrics.	Empty tank, check plug/flex.
Iron — rotary (calender)	Rotary cylinders.	Sheets, table linen, flat items.	Unplug, leave to cool.
Washing machines Twin-tub	Washing tank Rinse/spin drum.	Small loads — can boil.	Clean tank and drum. Dry. Check plug/flex.
Automatic front/ top load	Automatic wash, rinse and spin sequence, variable.	Light industrial use — can prewash.	Clean inside and detergent tray. Check outlet hose, flex/plug.

Type	Fitments	Purpose	Care/maintenence
Rotary washer	Semi-manual operation (only washes).	Industrial use – standard loads. Can boil.	Wash drum, check outlet and inlet hose taps.
Industrial automatic	Preset wash and rinse programmes.	Commercial and industrial loads.	Switch off, wipe out. Clean detergent inlet and filters.
Driers Spin-drier	Hose outlet, rubber top disc.	Spins water from fabrics, light use.	Unplug, check plug/flex and hose.
Water extraction	Top disc, water outlet pipe.	Water removal by a rotating drum – industrial use.	Switch off. Wipe out. Check outlet pipe.
Tumble-drier (domestic/industrial size)	Filter, hose and air outlet.	Removal of moisture by heated air and a tumble motion.	Switch off. Clean filter and air outlet hose.
Drying cabinet	Racks for linen, heating element.	Airing linen – domestic use.	Unplug, check flex/plug, and heating elements.

Criteria for the selection of laundry equipment

- The amount of space available, and the services and drainage available.
- The amount and type of articles to be laundered.
- The type of fabrics and the time available.
- The capital costs and running costs, guarantees.
- The ease of use and minimum maintenance requirements.
- The availability of suitable staff.

Household linens

Table-cloths and napkins

- Cotton is still the most usual material used, although man-made fabrics with polyester or terylene are sometimes used. Cotton makes the laundering easier if a commercial laundry is used.
- Always ensure that the style and pattern is in continuous supply before purchasing.

A typical on-premise laundry

A calender

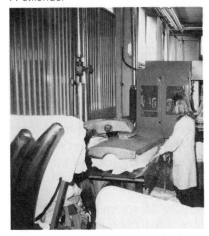

Steam pressing

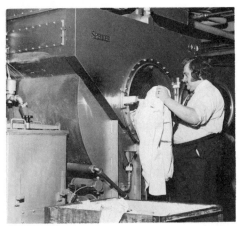

An industrial washing machine

- Stains are easier to remove from natural fabrics.
- Measure the table top and allow 55 cm all round for overhang and possible shrinkage.

Tea towels and glass cloths

- These are usually made of pure white linen, often with a coloured stripe at the sides.
- They will absorb water without leaving fluff on the glassware.
- Cotton cloths are not as absorbent or strong, and they tend to leave smears on the glassware.
- These cloths are used in the bars, still-rooms, wash-up areas and restaurants, and are usually laundered on the premises.

Towels

- These are made of looped pile, gripped by a woven backing. The wearing quality depends upon the backing being tightly woven, and a towel's absorbency depends upon the loop size and quality.
- Linen towels are very expensive and therefore are not often purchased.
- Cotton towels are usually used in residential establishments. They may be hot washed or boiled.
- Rayon towels are cheap but not very strong or thick.

Sheets and pillowcases

- *Linen* – these are the most expensive, very hard wearing but cold to the touch, and are not used in residential establishments.
- *Cotton* – these are hard wearing, comfortable and easily laundered. They are used in most residential establishments.
- *Twill/flanelette* – reasonably hard wearing, warm, and thicker than cotton. They are usually used as under-sheets. Easily laundered, heavy.
- *Terylene/polyester cotton* – reasonably comfortable and hard wearing. A thinner fabric than pure cotton. Always check before purchasing that a laundry can clean this fabric. It needs a cooler wash than cotton. Suitable for small units with an on-premises laundry.
- *Nylon* – cheap and very strong. It tends to be warm and to slip on the bed. It can cause static electricity. Not used in commercial residential units.

Types of fabric found in residential establishments

Name	Origin	Characteristics	Uses	Care
Wool	Sheep	Warm, woven into different types of fabric.	Carpets, blankets, upholstery, tailored uniforms.	Dry clean, may be moth-proofed, harmed by strong agents.
Silk	Silkworm	Smooth, not easily creased, expensive.	Luxury upholstery and curtains.	Specialist clean.
Cotton	Cotton plant	Cool, strong, woven to many different weights, comfortable, absorbent.	Bed linen, table kitchen linen, hospital blankets, unholstery, curtains, staff uniforms.	'Linen' may be boiled, starched and ironed as required, thicker items may be dry cleaned.
Linen	Stem of flax plant	Cool, strong, absorbent.	Glass cloths, table linen, curtains.	Hot wash, thin starch, hot iron, or dry clean.
Jute	Stem of jute plant	Strong fibres.	Carpet backing, linoleum backs.	Suction clean.
Rayon	Cellulose	Not very strong, blended with other fibres.	Furnishing fabrics, carpets.	Cool wash or dry clean.
Polyester, Terylene	Petroleum products	Very strong, not absorbent, made into varying types of fabric.	Table linen, staff uniforms, curtains, bed linen, filling for pillows/duvets.	Medium wash and iron if necessary.
Polyester/ cotton	Mixture of polyester and cotton fibres.	Warm to feel, soft, woven to different weights of fabric, strong.	Uniforms of all types, bed linen, upholstery, curtains.	Medium wash and iron if necessary.
Polymide, Nylon	Petroleum products	Strong, varying weights and textiles.	Trimming for uniforms, poor-quality bed linen.	Medium wash, creases easily, drip dry.
Acrilan, Courtelle, Dralon	Petroleum products	Warm feel, versatile fabrics.	Blankets, upholstery imitation — cotton, velvet and wool.	Cool wash or dry clean.

Upholstery

The base of upholstered furniture is a frame of wood, metal or plastic, on to which padding is fixed. Traditionally springs are attached to the frame, with hessian casing and wadding placed in layers to give softness. Some seats are constructed with horizontal tension springs or webbing fixed to the frame. Removable cushions are then placed on top of the springs, usually cut from latex or plastic foam blocks. If a plastic frame is used the upholstery is placed directly onto the plastic and fixed with adhesive.

Fillings for upholstery
- Animal hair – expensive; may be mixed with sisal fibres; fairly strong.
- Flock – waste rags and wool; cleaned before use.
- Feathers – these are down feathers that are specially treated; warm.
- Polyester – a soft, non-allergic filling.
- Latex foam – resilient and very durable.
- Plastic foam – very resilient and durable; highly inflammable; when it burns it gives off dangerous fumes.

Always check that upholstered furniture has passed the Upholstery Furniture (Safety) Regulations 1980 test. All safe items of furniture have a label attached to the frame, indicating that they have passed the flame tests.

Criteria for the selection of furnishings

The following points should be considered prior to selection:

Effect
Colour – should blend with existing schemes and not dominate.
Texture – decide upon the effect that the weave is to create.
Pile – this can be used to create a luxury effect.
Comfort – should be soft to the touch, never rough and course.

Heat
Fading – should not be damaged by sunlight or smoke.
Insulation – some fabrics have heat retention properties.
Flammability – should be resistant to fire and excess heat.

Wear
Strength – should be strong enough for the purpose for which it is intended.
Resistant – should be resistant to insect infestation.
Appearance – crease resistant properties are an asset.

Fluffing – select a fabric that is not liable to fluffing.
Weave – loose weaves will 'pull' easily, spoiling the effect.

Maintenance
Cleaning – choose a fabric that is easily cleaned.
Stains – select a fabric that is resistant to stains.
Linings – these should be compatible with the main fabric.
Resistant – select a fabric which is strong enough for the anticipated wear.
Cost – choose a fabric which will give value for money.

Curtains

All curtains should be properly lined. This helps to reduce fading and draughts, and makes the curtains hang better. It also helps to insulate the building.

If there is a radiator under the window-sill, the curtains should be short to allow the heat to come into the room.

Size
• Allow one and a half times the total width to be curtained (including the wall at the sides of the area).
• Allow the total length to be curtained and add an allowance for the heading and hems.
• Calculate the tape by using the total width of fabric. The tape is gathered up after it has been sewn on to the fabric.

Pattern
• Any design should be evenly placed across/down the curtains, so that only a small amount of fabric is wasted when cutting the fabric.
• There are various types of gathering tapes now available. Some will give a high heading, some a regular pleating effect and some are random gathering types. These should be considered and selected to suit the style which is being created.

Blinds

These are useful for keeping the strong glare of the sun from rooms and therefore for preventing overheating in hot weather. They also give privacy and yet allow light and air into the room.

Venetian blinds
• These are made from slats of aluminium or plastic in a variety of colours and nylon chords; they are hung vertically.
• They can be adjusted to admit light and air at the same time as

shading the room and giving privacy to the occupants.
- They are frequently used in areas such as offices, shops, foyers, reception areas, and in hospitals.
- Some are now being made of fibreglass material, with a woven finish. They are expensive but do create a pleasant finish to the room. These are hung horizontally and therefore open from side to side.

Roller blinds
- These can be made-to-measure for any size of window.
- They are made of glazed cotton or linen.
- These blinds roll up to the top of the window on a spring mechanism; this makes them liable to break if they are used frequently.
- They create a pleasant effect as they may be any colour or design, but they are not very strong for industrial use.

Methods of cleaning blinds
Any of the following methods may be used:

- A neutral detergent, sponge cloth to damp clean the slats.
- A foam-spray cleaner to remove grease marks.
- The entire blind removed and immersed in water, then rehung.

Assessment activities

1(a) List the types of cleaning agent which are used in your place of training or employment.
 (b) Analyse their effectiveness and draw a bar chart to indicate the detergents used and the types of surface that they are used to clean.

2(a) Clean some items of silver using the Polivit method.
 (b) Compare the process with another silver cleaning method. Discuss your conclusions.

3(a) Make up a divan bed using clean linen.
 (b) Time this process and count the number of times that you walk around the bed. Remake the bed using a revised method to reduce the time.

4(a) List the types and categories of linen that are laundered at your place of training or work.
 (b) Note their fabric composition and then recommend how these items should be cleaned/laundered to produce a good finish.

5(a) Find out the retail price of a complete set of bed clothes for a single divan bed.
 (b) List ways that these expensive items may be stored and controlled in residential establishments.

Unit 4:

Cleaning Equipment and Methods

The selection of cleaning equipment

The following points should be considered:

Efficiency

- The task to be completed, and the type of surface to be cleaned.
- The size of the area to be cleaned.
- The standard of finish required.

Economy

- The cost of the equipment, to purchase or to hire/lease.
- The additional tools and attachments which will be necessary.
- The type and cost of any cleaning agents that will be used.
- The running costs of using the equipment.

Staff

- The amount of effort needed to use the equipment.
- The size and weight of the equipment and of the additional tools.
- The type of controls and their ease of use.
- The ability of staff to use the equipment safely.

Departmental

- The size of the storage area that it will need.
- The servicing and parts replacement arrangements.
- The training requirements for staff to use the equipment.
- The ease of maintenance.

Management questions

- Will it replace another cleaning process, so reducing cleaning time and costs?
- Will it replace existing equipment, so reducing future requirements?
- What is the life expectancy of the machine/equipment? This amount should be written into the depreciation account.
- Will the existing staff be capable of operating the equipment/machines after training? What will the cost of this training be?

Types of equipment

These may be grouped as follows:

Manual	Electrical
brooms, brushes, dust-control mops, wet floor mops, dusters, cloths, buckets, wringer buckets, spray bottles, carpet sweepers, dustpans, trolleys.	dry suction cleaners, wet and dry suction cleaners, floor scrubbing machines, floor polishing machines, floor spray extraction machines, high-speed floor cleaning machines, high-pressure washers, floor suction sweepers.

Safety of electrical equipment

General

- Have the BEAB mark of safety.
- Have equipment serviced regularly by qualified electricians.
- Replace all frayed flexes.
- Replace broken or cracked plugs.
- Use the correct size fuses.
- Never overload the sockets.
- Never use portable electric fires.
- Switch off and unplug televisions when not in use.
- Switch off wall sockets when not being used.
- Use extension leads only in an emergency; they may cause accidents.

Supervision

- Adequate training of all staff.
- Effective supervision of all staff.
- Use work method charts and instruction cards for all staff, to ensure safe working practice.
- Check flex and plugs regularly.
- Never allow staff to trail flexes across a room.
- Never allow appliances to come into direct contact with water.
- Ensure that all equipment is cleaned and properly stored after use.

Fuses

- The fuse is the weakest link in the electrical circuit. Therefore, if the circuit is overloaded, the fuse will 'blow', breaking the circuit.
- Plugs have a small cartridge fuse inside. The size of this should

be suited to the particular appliance and the amount of electricity that it will use.

- 3 amp fuses will be suitable for domestic appliances, such as food mixers, hair-driers, radios, televisions.
- 13 amp fuses will be necessary for domestic appliances which use more electricity, such as heaters, suction cleaners, spin-driers.
- If in any doubt, always check with a qualified electrician before using the appliance.

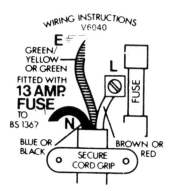

An electric plug

Manual equipment

Type	Characteristics	Area of use	Care
Soft broom	Bristle or nylon head.	Interior floors.	Remove fluff; wash occasionally in warm detergent water; rinse in cold water, hang up to dry and when not in use.
Hard broom	Wood and bristle.	Interior floors.	
Yard broom	Long, stiff bristles.	Exterior areas.	
Hand brush (soft)	Nylon or bristle.	With a dustpan.	
Hand brush (firm)	Stiff nylon or bristle.	Edges of carpet.	
Toilet brush	Nylon in own holder.	Toilet pans.	Wash, sterilise.
Scrubbing brush	Bristle or nylon.	Extra 'wet' areas.	Wash and drain dry.
Yard scrubbing broom	Long-handled, short stiff bristles.	Interior floor scrubbing.	Wash and drain dry, hang up when not in use.

Type	Characteristics	Area of use	Care
Dry dust control			
Impregnated mop	Cotton, oblong head.	Dust control.	Wash/reimpregnate.
Static mop	Polyester/cotton, oblong head.	Dust control on floors and stairs.	Wash and dry head and replace.
Short-handled static mop	Polyester, curved head – cylindrical.	Ledges, shelves, dust control.	Wash and dry head.
Disposable mop	Thin, woven fabric – fits to handle.	Infection/dust-control areas, hospitals.	Remove head and place in incinerator. Clean the head and handle.
Wet floor cleaning			
Short-head mop	Cotton strands, with strainer bucket.	Interior floors – wet cleaning.	Rinse well and hang up to dry.
Kentucky mop	Long cotton strands, with wringer bucket.	Large interior floors, wet/wash.	Rinse well and hang up to dry.
Detachable mop heads	Cotton heads, with a wringer bucket.	Infection control areas, floor wash.	Remove heads sterilise, dry and replace.
Cellulose mops	Sponge detachable.	Small floor areas.	Rinse well, hang up.
Buckets			
Twin with wringer	Two sections and wringer attached.	Wash and rinse solutions, long-headed mop.	Empty, wash out and dry thoroughly.
Single wringer	Bucket with wringer.	Long-headed mop.	Rinse and dry.
Single with strainer	Strainer over half of bucket top.	Short-headed mop.	Rinse and dry.
Dusters	Soft, yellow/checked.	Dry dusting.	Wash, hang up to dry.
Floor cloth	Absorbent, strong cotton.	Small areas.	Wash, hang up to dry.
Stockinette cloth	Thin, absorbent cotton.	Damp dusting.	Wash, hang up to dry.
Disposable cloth	Thin, woven fabric.	Infection control area.	Dispose of in incinerator.
Sponge cloth	Thin, cellulose sponge.	General purpose.	Wash, dry naturally.
Chamois-leather	Supple, thin leather.	Windows/glass.	Rinse, dry naturally.
Scrim	Thin, woven linen.	Windows/glass.	Rinse, dry naturally.

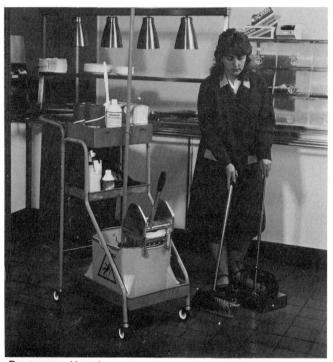

Dustpan and brush

Mop and wringer bucket

74

Type	Characteristics	Area of use	Care
Spray bottles	Lightweight, plastic, fine nozzle.	Damp dusting to disperse the detergent.	Empty after use. Clean the nozzle. Label it according to purpose.
Cleaner's trolley	Fitted with shelves, hooks, areas for all equipment that will be required, sack for refuse, buckets for water.	Mobile cleaning to enable the cleaners to take all their equipment to the work place.	Empty and clean all the shelves and buckets, check the castors, restock ready for the next day, dispose of refuse.
Carpet sweeper	Lightweight for carpets.	Emergency use in lounge and restaurant.	Empty the dust box, check the wheels.

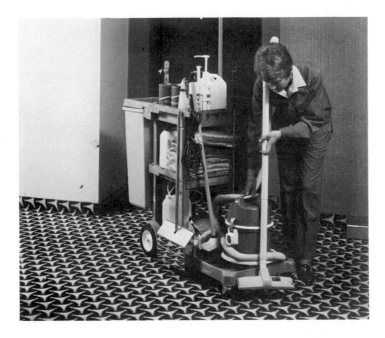

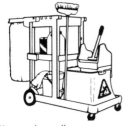  

Cleaner's trolley

Equipment storage

The store-room

- This should be situated near the work area to minimise loss or damage to the equipment, and to encourage staff to use the correct item of equipment for each task.
- All equipment should be clearly coded to allow tools to be used in the correct manner and to ensure efficient stock control (see equipment record card below); staff will be able to identify which tools fit each piece of equipment.
- Store-rooms should be the definite responsibility of a particular staff member and should be kept clean, tidy and well organised at all times. They should be locked when not in use to ensure efficient stock control (see equipment stock card below).
- Adequate shelving and hooks should be provided for the equipment to prevent damage to items and to encourage orderly storage of items.
- Equipment storage rooms should be well lit and ventilated, and should have areas suitable for cleaning/washing/drying equipment.

Equipment Record Card				
Item	Code	Location	Serviced	Checked
Suction cleaner	A	Room 314	August 1986	(supervisor's
Attachments—hose	A1	314		signature)
brush	A2	314		
nozzle	A3	314		
tube	A4	314		

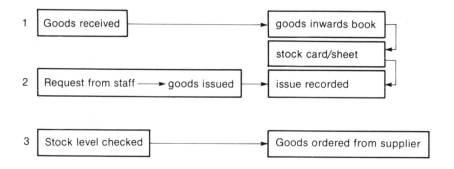

Issue procedure

Equipment Stock Card *Item* Duster – checked *Supplier* A. Bell & Sons			*Code* CD 15 *Maximum stock* 150 *Reorder level* 50	
Date	Inwards	Unit cost	Issued to	Balance
1.8.86 8.8.86 9.8.86	100	£ .20	10–D. Batch 15–A. Coat	150 150 140

Electrical equipment

Type	Fitments	Area of use	Care after use
Upright suction cleaner	Disposable dust bag. Hose, brushes and tube nozzles.	Carpeted areas, high dusting, upholstery, inaccessible areas.	Empty dust, clean all attachments, check flex, plug and wheels/brushes.
Cylinder suction cleaner	Extension tube and hose, brushes and nozzle.	Small areas only, stairs and high dusting.	As above.
Wet and dry suction tub/drum	Wet – water float. Dry – filter unit. Hose, tube, brushes, rubbers, nozzles.	Wet – pick up water and slurry after floor cleaning. Dry – high dusting.	Empty the drum, clean and dry. Clean the attachments, brush the dust filter. Check plug and flex.
Wet suction pick up	Adjustable head height.	Large areas which have been scrubbed or mopped.	Clean head, empty the tank and dry well, check plug and flex.
Suction/ polishing machine	Brushes, drive disc and pads.	Wooden floors which are polished.	Empty dust bag, clean attachments. Check flex and plug.
Scrubbing/ polishing machines – various speeds	Drive disc and pads of various types, brushes, water tank.	Floor areas that need polishing, buffing, scrubbing and burnishing.	Clean all pads and brushes, tank and disc. Dry all parts well. Hang up pads to dry. Check flex and plug.

Suction sweeper machines	Battery operated, seat for operative. Tanks and brushes.	Very large areas, dust and light debris removal.	Plug in to recharge the battery, empty tank, check brushes and inlet.
Scrubber/drier machines	Battery operated and seat for operative. Two tanks, filter, brushes.	Very large areas which need to be scrubbed and then dried.	Plug in to recharge the battery. Empty tanks, clean all parts, check filter.
Spray extraction machines.	Two tanks, hose, brush, spray nozzle.	Cleaning carpets and upholstery.	Empty and clean all parts, check plug, flex and spray nozzle.
High pressure washers	Tank, hose, tube, spray nozzle and pump.	Cleaning external and sanitary areas, walls and floors.	Empty and clean all parts, check battery, or plug and flex.

Dust control

Task – dry dusting

Areas
- Fixtures and fittings which are polished, varnished, painted, laminated or of vinyl material.

Equipment
- Dry, soft cloth and duster for horizontal dusting.
- Dry, soft brush or small mop for vertical dusting.

Method
1 Dust highest areas first, gradually working down to lower levels.
2 Work in a clockwise direction around the room.

Safety
- Eliminate any draughts and strong currents of air which will cause the dust to spread.
- Keep the duster or mop in contact with the surface at all times to prevent the scattering of dust.
- Bacteria live in dust and for this reason it is essential to wash equipment thoroughly after use.
- Methods and equipment must not be permitted to cause cross-infection.

Task – damp dusting

Areas
- Impervious furniture and fittings.

Equipment
- Cotton checked cloth.
- Hand-held spray bottle, filled with weak germicidal solution.
- Container for litter and refuse.

Method
1 Remove litter, refuse, ashtrays, plants and ornaments.
2 Spray small quantity of solution on to the cloth, then wipe the surface to be cleaned in overlapping strokes.
3 The edges and sides of tables and work-tops should be wiped after the tops.

Safety
- Use the correct dilution of germicidal detergent to ensure the maximum destruction of bacteria.
- The spray should be emptied and washed regularly, as the handle and nozzle quickly become sticky with prolonged use.
- The spray should always be directed on to the cotton cloth – never directly on to the surface or towards people.
- The cloth should be washed, rinsed and hung up to dry after use, to remove soiling and bacterial growth.

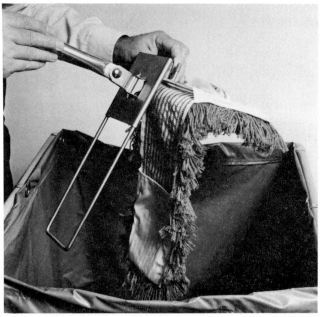

Dust control mopping – scissor action V-sweeper

Task – dust control mopping

Areas
- Dry, even floor surfaces which have no wet or sticky patches, e.g. corridors, classrooms, halls, gymnasiums, or any large areas.

Equipment
- Long-handled dust control mop, straight or scissor design, depending on the size of the area to be cleaned.
- Dustpan and soft brush.
- Container for litter and refuse.

Method
1 Keep the mop firmly on the floor surface all the time to allow the mop head to collect all the dust as it is worked across the floor surface.
2 Work the mop in a methodical manner up and down the complete floor area.
3 Overlap each stroke to ensure the complete collection of all dust.
4 Pay attention to the corners and awkward-shaped floor areas.
5 Collect litter with the dustpan and brush as is necessary.

Safety
- Always stand the mop upright when not in use, to prevent accidents.
- Mop heads should be removed and suction cleaned after use.
- When soiled, mop heads should be washed in germicidal detergent and rinsed well, then dried before further use.

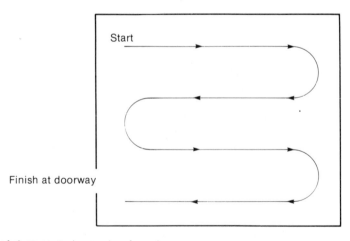

Method of dust control mopping for a large area

Task – sweeping

Areas
- Interior – floor surfaces where dry soiling deposits need to be removed.
- Exterior – patios, verandas, car-parks, paths, porch areas.

Equipment
- Interior – long-handled broom, soft bristle or nylon head; dustpan and brush to collect debris.
- Exterior – Long-handled broom, stiff bristles; shovel and brush to collect debris.

Method
1 Clear the area of as many obstructions as possible.
2 Sweep towards the exit area, using long, overlapping strokes.
3 Collect debris into dustpan at regular intervals.
4 Large areas should be swept in sections.

Safety
- Bacteria and contaminated debris will easily spread further unless the sweeping is carried out in a methodical, controlled manner.
- Brooms, dustpans and brushes should be washed in a germicidal detergent solution, then rinsed in cold water and hung up to dry.
- If at all possible, eliminate any draughts as these will cause the debris to spread further.

When sweeping, start at number 1 and work through to number 10.

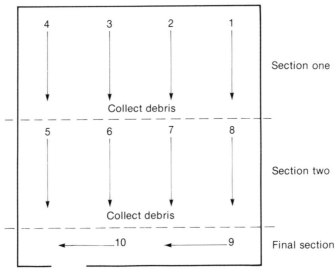

Method used for sweeping in sections

Scissor action V-sweeper

Dust mop

Floor cleaning

Task – wet/damp mopping

Areas
• Impervious surfaces, to remove light soiling.

Equipment
• Wet-floor warning notices.
• Two-section wringer bucket, one filled with hot detergent solution.
• One floor mop.
• Soft-headed broom and dustpan.
• Wet pick-up machine.

82

Method

1 Remove all items of furniture and small fittings if possible.
2 Sweep the area if the level of soiling is excessive.
3 Using one mop and the hot detergent solution, wet or damp mop the first section of the floor.
4 With the second mop and clear water, rinse this first section of floor.
5 Continue the process until the entire area has been cleaned.
6 A wet pick-up machine may be used if the floor surface needs to be dry immediately. It should be used to dry the floor, one section of the floor at a time.

Safety

- Change the water solution as frequently as the level of soiling dictates; the water should never be really dark and dirty.
- The dilution and type of detergent should be correct for the type of floor surface to be cleaned.
- The operative should wear safe, non-slip shoes.
- The equipment should be emptied and cleaned after use.
- The mops should be rinsed and hung up to dry. Dirty mops can be a breeding ground for bacteria, and can cause unpleasant odours.

When wet/damp mopping work from 1 to 16 (always finish by the doorway). Work on one section at a time. Complete the entire process before moving to the next section.

1	2	3	4
8	7	6	5
9	10	11	12
16	15	14	13

Damp mopping a large area

Task – floor scrubbing

Area

- Impervious floor surfaces which have a level of soiling or other contamination that makes scrubbing necessary, such as food preparation areas, laundries and cellars.

Equipment
- Warning notices for wet floor.
- Broom, and dustpan and brush.
- Electrical floor scrubbing machine with tank and brush attachments.
- Wet pick-up machine.
- Hand scrubbing brush and bucket for corners; detergent.

Method
1 Remove small items, and place warning notices in position.
2 Sweep floor to remove surface dirt.
3 Assemble floor cleaning machine, make up detergent solution and pour into the tank.
4 Scrub all corners by hand, using the small brush and bucket.
5 Scrub the floor area in sections, using sufficient detergent solution to ensure that the floor is adequately cleaned.
6 Pick up the slurry with the wet pick-up machine, one section at a time.
7 Rinse the floor if necessary and dry it with the wet pick-up.

Safety
- Check that the floor surface may be scrubbed without causing any damage.
- The detergent used and the concentration of the solution should be correct for the type of floor surface.
- The machines should be connected to separate electrical sockets, no extension leads should be used.
- The operative should wear safe, non-slip shoes.
- When the task is completed the machines should be cleaned and all detergent solution emptied out of the tank.
- The tank and brushes should be washed and hung up to dry.

Start at number 1 and proceed in sections to number 12. Pick up the slurry at the end of each section, before going on to scrub the next section of the floor.

12	7	6	1
11	8	5	2
10	9	4	3

Electric sockets

Method used for floor scrubbing

Window cleaning

Combined floor scrubber/dryer

Task – floor buffing

Areas
- Impervious floor surfaces which have been sealed, e.g. corridors, halls, classrooms, hospital floors.

Equipment
- High-speed polishing machine and buffing pads.
- Spray buff solution in spray bottle.
- Soft broom, dust control mop and container for litter.
- Floor cleaning warning signs.

Method
1 Remove all small items from the floor area.
2 Check the surface is free from fluff, litter, spillages or gum.
3 Assemble the machine and fill the spray bottle.
4 Spray a small section of the floor and buff that area, using the machine to create a shine on the floor area.

5 Continue to work across the floor in sections until the entire surface is clean and glossy. Change the pad as necessary.
6 Use the dust control mop to remove the resulting dust to finish.

Safety
- Ensure that the machine is assembled correctly.
- Place the floor-cleaning warning signs in position.
- Ensure that the spray solution is compatible with the floor seal.
- Spray very finely, as too much solution will eliminate the shine.
- The pads should be washed and drained dry after use.
- The machine should be cleaned and stored away properly.
- The operative should wear non-slip shoes.
- When spray buffing a corridor, work one side for the full length to enable the public to use the remaining half as required, then spray and buff up the second side of the corridor.
- Spray and buff one area at a time. Unplug the machine from the electric socket when the next one is obviously nearer.

When cleaning a corridor, work from sections 1 to 8, as shown.

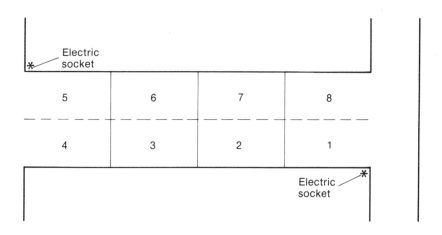

Method used for buffing a corridor

Suction cleaning (dry)

Areas
- Smooth, impervious surfaces which need to be free from dust particles, such as hospital floors, carpeted areas and upholstery items.

Equipment
- Suction cleaner, with attachments as required.
- Small, stiff hand brush.

Method
1 Pick up sharp, sticky items from the floor surface.
2 Remove small items from the floor area.
3 Brush the corners with a stiff hand brush to remove fluff.
4 Plug in the cleaner and work across the floor surface in a methodical manner, keeping the flex behind the machine.
5 Use the hose and small brush attachment to suction clean any upholstery and curtained areas.

Safety
- Ensure that the machine is switched off before plugging into the wall socket.
- Check that the dust container is empty before using the suction cleaner.
- Ensure that the flex does not trail over a large floor area, as this can cause accidents.
- Always empty the dust container after use and store the cleaner away properly.

Staircase cleaning

Areas
- Indoor staircases.

Equipment
- Dust control mop for impervious surfaces.
- Duster for banisters and hand rails.
- Suction cleaner, with brush and hose attachments for carpet area.
- Warning notices.

Method
1 Assemble equipment as appropriate.
2 Place warning notices at top and bottom of staircase.
3 Start at the top of the flight of stairs, work across the top tread, and then the rise.
4 Work across the second tread, and then the second rise.
5 Proceed in this manner until the complete flight has been cleaned.
6 Starting at the top of the flight of stairs again, dust the banisters, hand rails, brackets and skirting boards.
7 If using a dust control mop on a sealed staircase, start at the top of the flight of stairs and keep the dust control mop in contact with

the surface being cleaned at all times as the mop is worked down the flight of stairs.

Safety
- Place the warning signs where they may easily be seen.
- Clean and replace equipment after use. Empty the dust container.
- Never leave any equipment on the staircase.

Combined scrubbing/drying machine

Assessment activities

1(a) List the types of electrical cleaning equipment which are necessary to effectively clean your place of training.
 (b) Suggest alternative pieces of manual equipment which could produce a similar standard of cleanliness.
 (c) Discuss the differences between the results of these two methods.

2 Clean a window by three different methods and chart the results achieved, considering the following points:
(i) time taken (ii) effort required (iii) equipment used (iv) finished effect.

3 Design new equipment stock cards for the cleaning equipment and agents which are used at your place of work or training.

4(a) Design a chart to indicate the use of a piece of electrical equipment.
 (b) Display your chart next to the piece of equipment to which it relates.

5(a) Write a work instruction card for a simple cleaning task.
 (b) Invite one of your group members to carry out the instructions you have written, while you analyse their work.

Unit 5:

Surfaces and Fittings

Wall coverings

The purpose of wall coverings is to protect the wall itself or to enhance the decorative appearance of the wall. There are numerous different coverings available; the main types are listed below.

Panels

These are made from plain or carved wood, which may be stained and varnished to protect the wood, or oiled to increase the natural beauty of the wood grain.

Care
- Dry dust regularly, paying particular attention to grooves, niches and ledges, as these will collect dust that quickly builds up with grease and dirt, which will spoil the colour of the wood.
- Apply wax polish or oil as necessary, taking care to brush well in the corners with a soft brush to remove any build up of dirt.

Tiles

These are made of sealed cork, smooth or patterned ceramics or mirrored.

Cork: always sealed and used to increase sound insulation; the natural cork colour and pattern creates an attractive finish.

Smooth ceramic: these tiles have a high gloss finish and are used in many food preparation areas, bathrooms, and cloakrooms; they are also used in sports areas and swimming pools and provide an impervious, easily cleaned wall surface.

Patterned ceramics: these tiles have a slightly uneven surface beneath the gloss finish; this makes them less suitable for industrial use, as they are more difficult to clean.

Mirror: these tiles are used to increase the light effect of an area, or to increase the impression of size and space.

Care
- Tiles may be washed, using a spray of hot water, a germicidal detergent and a soft cloth. They should be rubbed dry with a cloth to prevent water marks spoiling the effect.

Paper

These may be plain, embossed or vinyl coated. There are numerous plain and patterned papers available to enhance the appearance of a room or area.

Care
- Vinyl coated papers may be carefully wiped with a damp cloth to remove any marks.
- Marks may be removed from non-washable papers by gently rubbing the soiled area with a soft, clean eraser.
- Dust may be removed by suction cleaning or by using a soft wall brush.

Brick/stone

These may be used to create a rustic effect in bars and halls, and around fireplaces and in conservatories and porches.

Care
- Brick/stone work may be kept free from dust by using a suction cleaner. A small brush needs to be used in corners to keep these free from dust.

Wall protection methods

Walls need to be protected in high-traffic areas from marks, bumps and scratches. The base of walls needs to be adequately protected from heavy-duty floor cleaning machines.

Clear plastic
- Guards around light switches and door handles will prevent excessive soiling from finger marks.
- Sheets fixed on to staircases below the hand rail will prevent any scuff marks on walls.

Aluminium
- Corner guards fitted on areas of the walls where trolleys and wheelchairs are liable to knock the walls, e.g. corridors, landings near lifts.

Wood
- Skirting boards are fitted to protect the base of the wall and to eliminate draughts from the floor boards.
- Wooden strips fitted to protect the walls from the backs of chairs in rooms used for meetings, lessons, receptions.

Paint

There are numerous colours and types of paint available – a summary of the main types can be seen below. An expert interior decorator will be able to advise on any technical aspects.

Gloss

- This gives a shiny finish to wooden surfaces after treatment with an undercoat. Normally used for finish to skirting boards, doors, window-ledges and frames.

Egg shell

- This gives a semi-gloss finish and is often referred to as matt finish. It is easier to apply on wood surfaces than gloss paint. An undercoat, suitable for interior wooden surfaces, must be used.

Emulsion (water based)

- This is applied to walls and ceilings and is used to provide a smooth finish to plastered surfaces. It may be either a matt finish or a semi-gloss finish.

Primer

- This is for initial treatment of unpainted wood or metal before an undercoat is used.

Undercoat

- This helps to bind the gloss paint to the primed surface.

Exterior

- This paint is made with a fungicide to prevent mould growth. It is used on the exterior part of buildings.

Vinyl

- A strong finish is obtained with this type of paint, which is easy to keep elegant.

Special

- Special finishes are used for definite problem areas; they include anti-condensation, flame retardent, fluorescent, anti-graffiti, exterior metal areas.

Care
• Damp dust as required. Sand down and repaint areas which become flaked, stained or damaged in any way.

Windows

The treatment of windows requires as much thought and care as the covering of walls and floors. The effect to be created in any room may be determined by the choice of windows. The following points should be remembered:

• Light and air should not be excluded.
• Vision from within the room should not be obscured.
• Privacy of the occupants should not be restricted.
• Window treatment must be an integral part of the decor.
• Materials should be chosen with the following considerations:
  a) price,
  b) durability,
  c) resistance to fading,
  d) ease of maintainence washing.
• The outlook:
  a) if on to a street or building, vision nets will be required – for the occupants' privacy.
  b) if on to countryside area, nets may not be needed.

Care of vision nets

These should be washed regularly, since they will attract and hold dust in the weave/patterns. They should be folded and then soaked/washed in detergent with a biological enzyme, keeping the curtains folded all the time. They will need thorough rinsing, still folded, and should then be hung out to drip dry. This method will eliminate the need for pressing/ironing, as these nets are not easy to iron. It should be remembered that, since washing is a regular occurrence, spare pairs of curtains should be available.

The shape of windows

Sash or casement
Where two are close together on the same wall, it is often best to treat them as one and to curtain right across. This will create a warm appearance when the curtains are closed, and an even look when they are open.

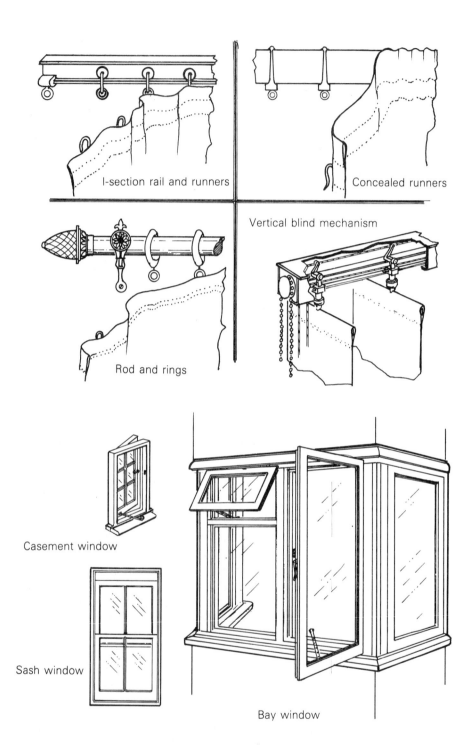

I-section rail and runners

Concealed runners

Vertical blind mechanism

Rod and rings

Casement window

Sash window

Bay window

Bay
The curtains may follow the curve, or thicker, floor-length ones may be drawn across the bay. This reduces the size of the room but it excludes draughts. The window may be made into a feature by fitting seats and, therefore, shorter curtains.

Picture
These are large expanses of window used to give unimpeded vision. The view should not be obscured. Any curtains should hang at the sides and be drawn by chords.

Curtain rails

There are various types available, as follows:

- Poles, made from varnished wood or plastic, with rings.
- Plastic rails, with plastic hooks concealed at the back.
- Metal rails, with plastic hooks which fix over the rail.

Glass

There are various types of finished glass which may be used in residential units, as follows:

Clear
- This is used in windows where maximum light is required.

Frosted
- This is used in windows where light is necessary but where vision needs to be restricted, in doors and in toilet and bathroom windows.

Safety glass
- This is made with sheets of wire incorporated in the glass. The wire prevents the glass falling if the pane is broken. For this reason, it is used for skylights and fire doors.

Toughened glass
- This is clear glass which has been processed in such a way that it will shatter into tiny fragments if the glass is broken, thereby eliminating any large, sharp pieces.

Security glass
- This is a safety glass which is toughened and laminated to make glass that is five times' stronger than normal.

Plate glass
- This provides clear, undistorted vision and is used in large glass windows, picture windows and shop windows.
- It is used for mirrors with a bevelled edge to eliminate sharp corners.
- It may be used for glass tops on furniture or glass shelves in display cabinets. The edges must be bevelled.

Double glazed
- This is used to increase the insulation in window frames. Two panes of glass are sealed and assembled in the frame, allowing a thin layer of air to be permanently trapped.

Cross section of double glazing

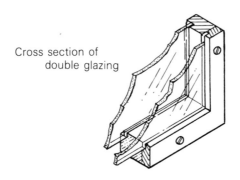

Methods of cleaning glass

Tools
- Warm water with neutral detergent and a set of window washing and squeegy tools (see page 85). The washing head has a soft cotton cover over a cylindrical frame. The rinsing head has a rubber blade, which will remove all moisture from the glass.

Chamois
- The leather is a natural product which is expensive to purchase. It is used with hot, clear water, wrung out until it is nearly dry, then wiped firmly over the entire glass area.

Synthetic leather
- This has the same effect as chamois but is far less expensive. It is useful for removing smears and finger marks from doors.

Materials used to make furniture

Plastics

Inexpensive, lightweight and easily cleaned. Expanded polyurethane and rubber foam is used for upholstery, bonded PVC for imitation leather finishes. Plastics are used to coat metal frameworks. Reinforced moulded plastic is used for chairs and tables.

Leather

Hide is very expensive and must be kept supple and soft. It is difficult to clean and may crack if not well cared for.

Metals

These are used for frameworks and for complete items of furniture. For example, iron, steel, aluminium and chrome are used, with various finishes. Brass and copper are also used mainly for handles and occasional table tops.

Glass

This is used for table tops. Plate glass, with toughened, shatter-proof qualities and bevelled edges is normally used.

Wood

Many types of wood are used to make furniture. They include the following: beech, birch, oak, deal, elm, mohagony and teak.

Wood needs a protective finish if used for furniture. Any of the finishes listed below may be used:

- Wax – a mix of beeswax and turpentine paste. It gives low protection against water and heat.
- Oil – a mix of linseed oil and turpentine solution. It gives little protection against water and heat.
- French polish – made from shellac dissolved in spirit. This gives poor resistance to heat and water and will scratch.
- Nitro-cellulose – a matt or full gloss finish may be obtained. This has fair resistance to wear.
- Synthetic resin – melamine coating. This gives an impervious coat, with good resistance to heat, water and abrasions.
- Polyurethane varnish – gives a high gloss finish with an impervious finish, and gives good protection against heat, water and scratches.

Veneer

Veneering is an economical and sound method of producing well-finished furniture. Costly, hard wood or plastic sheets imitating wood are glued to a base of soft wood, chipboard, blockboard or plywood, thus creating the desired finished appearance with reduced cost and furniture of a lighter weight. This furniture will be less liable to warp in heat than similar, solid wood types.

Paint

This may be gloss, emulsion, matt finish or vinyl based and has a relatively short life, since it is liable to crack or chip off the wooden surface. It provides reasonable protection against heat and moisture.

The selection of furniture

The following points should be considered before selecting furniture:

Purpose

- Fixed furniture can make cleaning easier and can reduce the dust 'trap' areas behind and above furniture.
- Free-standing furniture will give greater versatility to the effect created in the room.
- If the furniture is fitted flush to the floor it will make daily cleaning quicker and easier.
- Furniture on legs makes cleaning a slower process, and the legs can dent the carpet surface.
- Furniture on castors is easily moved around for cleaning and for repositioning within the room.
- The size and height of the furniture should be chosen with consideration given to the size of any existing fittings.

Materials

- The choice of materials will be influenced by the effect to be created in the room.

- The colour and texture of the furniture should blend with or complement the colour scheme.
- The furniture should be constructed in a material which is suitable for the anticipated uses.

Design

- The furniture should be of a design that is compatible with the existing furnishings.
- The design of furniture should be suitable for the anticipated uses.
- The furniture should be well constructed with a strong frame.
- The construction method should make future repairs possible.
- All edges and surfaces should be smooth and well joined.
- The legs, handles and drawers should be well balanced and strong.
- The doors should have well constructed hinges which are capable of holding the weight.
- The British Standard Kitemark will indicate an acceptable standard.

Maintenance

- The furniture should be easy to clean.
- Free-standing furniture should be easily moved.
- The interior sections of the furniture should be easily accessible for cleaning purposes.

Care and cleaning of furniture

The following points should be remembered:
- Avoid scratching and banging furniture.
- Always remove soiling as soon as possible.
- Rotate the position of the furniture in the room to avoid persistent wear, sun damage or heat damage.
- Clean the furniture regularly and thoroughly, including the inside and the back.
- Maintain the furniture properly; check the springs, legs, castors, handles and supports; worn parts need to be replaced.

The table below gives details of how to care for and clean damaged or soiled furniture.

Material	Likely faults or damage	Remedy/care
Polished wood	Scratched surface. Heat or water marks.	Colour scratched area, repolish. Rub mark with metal polish until the mark disappears, then repolish.
Varnished wood	Split or flaked varnish.	Rub with fine sand paper, then revarnish the damaged area, or it may be necessary to strip and revarnish entire item.
Painted wood	Heat marks, resin stains, flaked or chipped paint.	Treat with fine sand paper, and repaint.
Moulded plastic	General darkening of the colour. Loosening of the frame.	Clean with neutral detergent solution and a sponge. Rebolt sections to the frame.
Melamine coated	Heat marks. Edging coming away.	Use a non-scratch cleanser to remove the burn colour. Use strong glue to refix strip.
Glass	Scratched or chipped at the edges.	Send to a glass specialist to have the edge rebevelled.
Painted metal	Chipped, dented, bent. Rubber 'feet' missing.	Repaint and straighten. Replace rubber ferrules.
Copper/brass	Metal polish caught in moulding. Tarnished.	Brush mouldings, then clean with metal polish. Buff up well.
Upholstered fabric	Crumbs in crevices. Darkened colour.	Suction clean with nozzle. Damp clean with shampoo, suction clean when dry.

Space-saving furniture

Versatility of use in many residential and public areas means that consideration must be given to space saving and easy storage of extra furniture. Normal items used are as follows:

- Sliding doors and room dividers.
- Folding tables and chairs.
- Table extensions and leaves.
- Cantilever shelves, tables and seats.
- Stackable chairs and tables.
- Fold-away beds.

Selection of these items will depend upon the intended purposes to which the room/furniture is to be put. For example, a bedroom suite may be changed into a small, private dining room or meeting room with the use of a fold-away bed unit and a table that may be extended. Tables and chairs are needed for meetings and large receptions, whereas the same function room may be required without these items for an exhibition or a dance. The use of this method of maximum room usage will increase the turnover of business and should therefore be encouraged.

See page 104.

Beds

There are many different types of bed available. Those listed below will give an indication of the main differences between the various types and uses.

Hospital
- Adjustable height and angles.
- Mobile – castors, which must be lockable.
- Metal frames, which must have the minimum number of joints and ridges.
- Mattress – pocketed sprung, encased in impervious plastic cover.

Divan (base)
- Box-edged – springs encased in firm wooden case, easy to clean.
- Spring edged – spring whole width of base, not very strong.

Divan (mattress)
- Posture sprung – best quality, even wearing over entire surface.
- Pocketed sprung – average quality, hard wearing.
- Rubber foam – soft and hygienic, different thicknesses available.

Wood/spring base
- Metal frame – wire mesh held tight between the frame.
- Wood frame – wooden slats held between the frame, a very firm base.

Living/sleeping

Small meeting

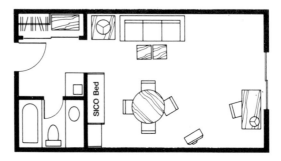

Group meeting

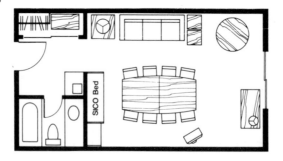

A convertible room

104

This type of base is less expensive and stronger than a divan base, and is often used in schools and halls of residence, as the whole bed is raised well above the ground and is easier to clean underneath.

Pillows
- Down – soft and expensive, must be specialist cleaned.
- Latex foam – good, semi-firm feel, washable, reasonable price.
- Terylene – medium-soft, expensive, washable.

Cleaning and care of beds

Daily – make the bed with clean linen as required, dust the head-board and frame.
Weekly – strip the bed, suction clean the base and mattress, turn it over, check the legs, castors and the head-board.
Hospital – these beds are changed as necessary by the nursing personnel; the entire bed is cleaned between patients and as required at other times.

Floors

Type	Area of use	Care	Characteristics
Wood – strip block, parquet.	Gymnasiums. Library. Dance floors.	Daily dust removal. Buff as required.	Sealed hard wood. Natural colour.
Cork – tiles, carpet.	Hospitals – quiet areas. Light traffic areas.	Daily dust removal. Avoid contact with water.	Permanent seal must be applied. Quiet and warm.
Linoleum – sheet.	Domestic use. Corridors. Hallways.	Daily dust removal. Damp wash.	Excess water will damage.
Magnesite – jointless.	Store areas. Industrial uses.	Daily dust removal. Damp mop.	Damaged by acids, alkalis and water.
Thermoplastic – sheet, tiles.	Hospitals. Schools. Corridors, classrooms. Shops, offices.	Daily dust removal. Damp mop. Buff as required.	Sealed surface. May crack, easy to replace, noisy/cold.
Polyvinyl chloride – sheet, tiles.	Hospital wards. Halls. Libraries. Reception areas.	Daily dust removal. Damp mop. Buff as required.	Sealed. Very quiet.

Type	Areas of use	Care	Characteristics
Rubber – sheet, tiles.	Hospitals. Libraries. Entrances. Corridors.	Daily dust removal. Wet mop, wet pick-up.	May be sealed. Quiet. Warm.
Rubber-ribbed – sheet, link mats.	Interior walkways. Airports. Shopping halls. Sports centres.	Wet clean by machine. Neutral detergent. Wet pick-up.	Quiet, hard wearing. Non-slip.
Marble – slabs, tiles.	Large halls in public buildings.	Wet mopping with neutral detergent.	Cold, noisy, will bruise. Expensive.
Terrazzo – seamless.	Entrance halls. Shops. Corridors.	Wet mop with a neutral detergent.	Very durable. Cold. noisy.
Stone – slabs.	Public buildings. Churches. Markets. Old buildings.	Sweep, wet mop or light scrub. Wet pick-up.	Uneven finish. Cold, noisy.
Quarry tiles.	Toilets. Changing rooms. Kitchens. Storerooms. Laundries. Halls.	Wash with high pressure washer or wet mop. Wet pick-up.	Impervious. Cold, noisy. Slippery when wet.
Ceramic – tiles	Cloakrooms. Toilets. Foyers. Swimming-pool.	Wet mop/light scrub. Wet pick-up, dry off.	Impervious, many colours and designs.
Concrete – seamless.	Loading bays. Exterior paths and steps. Factories. Garages. Fire escapes.	Sweep, scrub by machine, or use high-pressure wash. Wet pick-up.	May be sealed if indoors, Noisy, cold. May create dust.
Granolithic – seamless/slabs.	Laundries. Cloakroom. Corridors. Storeroom.	Wash/light scrub. Buff as required.	Sealed. Noisy, cold. Slippery when wet.
Metal link.	Escalators. Moving pathways.	Damp clean any marks. Dry suction clean.	Very hard wearing. Never get wet.

Antistatic floorings

These are manufactured to eliminate the hazards of fire or explosions. They include such types as terrazzo, magnesite, linoleum, rubber, PVC and tiles. There are metal strips or wire mesh layed in the flooring to give antistatic properties. The uses are in operating theatres, X-ray rooms and computer rooms. Antistatic carpets should be made of natural fibres to prevent a build up of static electricity.

Criteria for the selection of floorings

The following points should be considered before selecting a floor surface:

Area
- The size of the floor and the use to which it will be put.
- The effect that is to be created, the colour and comfort level.
- The anticipated type and level of traffic in the area.
- The adjacent types of flooring/area.
- The cost, and the sub-floor properties.

Wear
- The strength of the flooring, and its resistance to noise.
- The flammable properties of the flooring.
- The resistance to staining and fading, and/or heat.
- The flooring's resistance to insect infestation.
- Should the flooring have non-slip properties, and be impervious?

Maintenance
- The ease of cleaning and the time required to clean.
- The frequency of the cleaning process and its cost.
- The equipment necessary to clean the flooring and the capabilities of the existing staff.
- The necessity of any additional treatments, such as floor sealing.
- The life expectancy of the flooring and the cost per annum to the depreciation account.

Carpets

Type	Uses	Care	Characteristics
Pile – Wilton, Brussels. Wool, or wool and synthetics.	The most expensive type – luxury uses. In lounges and areas where hard wear and comfort are essential.	Good underlay. Suction clean. Spot clean if required.	Warm, luxurious. Close, soft pile. Long lasting if well cared for. Many designs.
Tufted – Axminster. Wool or wool and synthetics.	Industrial uses, e.g. bedrooms. Less expensive than Wilton.	Good, thick underlay is necessary. Suction clean. Shampoo.	Tufted cut on hessian. May have foam backing. Plain/patterned.
Woven – sisal	Very hard wearing. Corridors, halls, common rooms, offices.	Thick underlay is essential. Suction clean.	Very tough, hard. Slippery if on stairs.
Cord or bonded – nylon, acrylic, polyester on a foam backing.	Light industrial use.	Good, thick underlay. Suction clean. Shampoo/spot clean.	Ridged or patterned finish. Tends to harbour dust and fluff.
Carpet tiles – pig hair backed on to jute. Synthetics on backings.	Hard wearing if of good quality. In offices, halls, corridors, bars, common rooms.	Suction clean. Lift up if soiled and wash as necessary, then replace.	May be rough to the touch. Very durable. One or two may be replaced if damaged.

Carpet underlay

The purpose of this is to protect the carpet from pressure from either the floor itself or the footwear above. It also prolongs the life of the carpet, reduces the draught from the sub-floor area and makes the carpet warmer and softer to the touch.

Types of underlay which are available are noted below.

Felt
- Made of hair or cotton, it is of medium quality. It creates dust and is not washable. It will wear thin with constant traffic in places such as doorways.

108

Felt rubber
- This is felt backed on to rubber. Warm and reasonably strong. Not washable, and will create dust.

Foam
- May be backed on to hessian. Strong, clean, washable.

Paper
- Thin and has limited life. Inexpensive. Will wear out in walkways.

The quality of carpets

The quality will depend upon the following:

- The type of fibre used to make the carpet.
- The type of weave/pile, and the thickness.
- The quality of carpet construction.
- The classification of the carpet, and its grade.

Carpet grades are as follows:

- Light contract – used for domestic and bedroom area.
- Medium contract – used for residential areas.
- Heavy contract – used for heavy traffic areas, e.g. entrances.

The criteria for the selection of carpets is as follows:

- Consider the amount of wear that it will receive.
- Identify the type of sub-floor and select the appropriate underlay.
- Choose a colour and design which are suitable for the area.
- Decide upon the type of carpet required – fitted or square.
- Consider its resistance to stains and to fading/heat.
- Select within the costs available.

Carpets are fitted to the floor by the following methods:

- Ring and pin, or pin and socket – when carpets need to be lifted regularly, such as in conference/dance halls.
- Gripper strips – when carpets are fitted wall-to-wall.
- Bars or strips – made of wood or metal and used in doorways to join carpets.
- Adhesive strips – used to join two or more sections together.

Care of carpets

Daily dust removal
- To ensure that crumbs, bacteria, etc., are removed before they cause any damage to the carpet.

- To increase the life of the carpet, as grit will damage the fibres and the back.
- To retain the acoustic value of the carpet – if it is clogged up with dirt it will become hard.
- To retain its original colour, texture and effect.

Weekly attention
- Spot clean as necessary to remove marks. This will reduce the necessity to shampoo the carpet.
- Use a stiff nylon brush around the edges and corners to remove all fluff and dust before using a nozzle attachment on the suction cleaner.

Special occasional attention
- Clear the floor area completely and shampoo or use a carpet extraction machine to clean the fibres in the carpet. Leave well ventilated to dry, then suction clean.

Assessment activities

1(a) Make a collection of different types of wallpaper and suggest a suitable use for each type that you have collected.
 (b) Mount your collections to create a wall chart.

2(a) Measure a set of windows and then estimate the cost of curtaining that would be required.
 (b) Choose a suitable fabric and curtain rail fitting for the windows.
 (c) Display your work.

3(a) Look around the premises where you are employed or trained and list the types of glass that are used in doors and windows.
 (b) Discuss the use of glass on the premises and suggest the reasons why glass is used.

4(a) List the types of material that are used in the furniture at your place of work or training.
 (b) Discuss their characteristics and write a cleaning schedule for the types of furniture.

5(a) Identify the types of floor surface that are to be found at your place of work or training.
 (b) Note any damage or faults on the floors and recommend an alternative floor surface for each area, giving reasons for your choice.

Unit 6:

House Services Control

Work schedules

Before deciding on a work schedule the following points need to be considered:

- Decide which surfaces and items need to be cleaned.
- Identify the materials the items are made of.
- Select the equipment and cleaning agent suitable for each task.
- Decide how frequently each cleaning task should be completed.

An example of a daily work schedule for a lounge can be seen below.

FREQUENCY	Daily	LOCATION Lounge	NAME
Task	*Time*	*Equipment/cleaning agent*	*Method*
1 Ventilate.	1 min	—	Adjust curtains and blinds. Open windows.
2 Remove litter.	2 min	Waste-paper sack/trolley.	Remove old newspapers, dead flowers, used crockery/glasses empty ashtrays.
3 Adjust ventilation.	1 min	—	Check heating and air flow level. Adjust the windows.
4 Furniture.	3 min	Yellow duster. Polish and soft cloths.	Dry dust. Apply polish if this is necessary.
5 Skirting boards and paintwork.	2 min	Hand-held spray with a detergent solution and a soft, checked cloth.	Damp dust, and remove all finger marks from doors, sills and ledges.
6 Upholstery, chairs, settees.	2 min	Straighten cushions. Yellow duster. Suction cleaner hose/brush.	Dry dust legs and wooden parts. Suction clean as necessary.
7 Carpet/floor.	2 min	Suction cleaner.	Remove dust with suction cleaner.
8 Check the room.	1 min	—	Replace flowers/plants. Lay out current newspapers, clean ashtrays, and waste-paper baskets.

Work schedules should give any cleaning personnel the precise information necessary to clean a given area, including the length of time that this cleaning should take, the cleaning equipment and agents to be used, and the correct sequence to be followed when carrying out the cleaning.

Using work schedules

When using work schedules to plan the tasks that should be completed by staff it is possible to do the following:

- Predict the time which will be taken to complete each task.
- Plan the sequence of tasks to be completed.
- Itemise the equipment necessary to complete the tasks.
- List the cleaning agents to be used when cleaning the room.
- Estimate the cleaning costs for any given period – a month, a year.
- Estimate the total cleaning times, giving the number of hours needed to clean the entire premises, on a daily basis.
- Work out staffing levels and staff rotas.
- Purchase the required cleaning agents in bulk.

Work schedules may be compiled for every area within the premises that needs to be cleaned on a regular basis. The sequence of tasks will vary according to the type of cleaning to be completed – daily, weekly or special.

The weekly cleaning tasks may be incorporated into the daily cleaning schedule by the following method:

1 Devise and write the daily cleaning schedule.
2 List the additional weekly cleaning tasks.
3 Divide these weekly tasks between the five days that the daily cleaning schedule covers per week.
4 Incorporate one weekly task into the daily cleaning schedule for each day. For example, daily clean the given area *and*, on the appropriate day, include the allotted weekly cleaning task.

Mondays – extra attention to all floors.
Tuesdays – high level dusting and walls.
Wednesdays – extra attention to all beds and upholstery.
Thursdays – extra cleaning of all sanitary appliances/fitments and areas.
Fridays – windows, frames and glass, and paintwork.

The times/situations when work schedules are useful are as follows:

- Staff not managing to complete work in the time allowed.
- Excessive use of cleaning agents.

- Cleaning not being completed to the required standard.
- Staff complaints concerning insufficient cleaning equipment.
- Cleaning equipment not replaced in correct store area.
- Staff becoming irritable and unhappy when they have finished their shift.
- Staff thinking that they are expected to complete more work than others employed to do the same tasks.

Inspection procedures

When a room is ready for occupation it should be checked by the assistant housekeeper or supervisor in the following manner:

- The room should be entered and the door closed.
- The first impression the room creates is the most important.
- Proceed slowly round the room in a clockwise direction and note any faults.
- Look high up, then at eye level, then table top level, then low down.
- All faults or soiled areas should be noted on a form similar to the one illustrated below.

Marks: 5 – excellent, 4 – good, 3 – acceptable, 2 – some soiling, 1 – unclean.

| Room number _____ Date _____ Time _____ | | |
| Staff name _____ Supervisor _____ | | |
Item/area	Mark	Action to be taken
Door		
Light fittings		
Windows – glass		
Windows – frame		
Ceiling		
Walls		
Upholstery – chairs		
Upholstery – head-board		
Beds – mattress		
Beds – made up ready		
Flat surfaces – table		
Flat surfaces – shelves		
Flat surfaces – mirror		
Floor – carpet		
Floor – surrounds		
Cupboards – chest of drawers		
Cupboards – wardrobe		

Room Inspection Form

Regular failures in the same area to be cleaned need to be investigated. They may be caused by (a) lack of staff training or lack of time, or (b) lack of equipment or agents for that task.

If room-maids and cleaning staff are made aware of the room inspection procedure, they will be more likely to clean the rooms to an acceptable standard.

During the room inspection the following questions need to be asked:

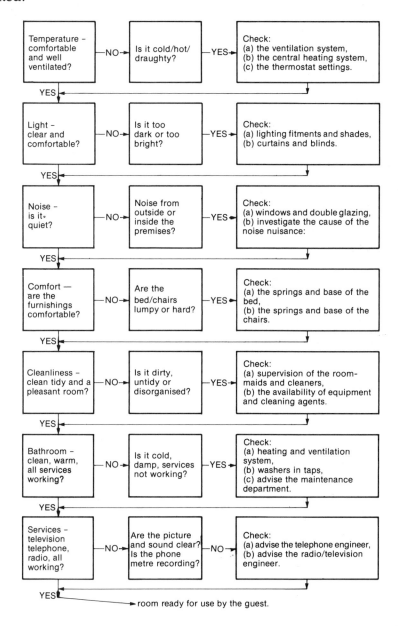

Maintenance

Preventative maintenance

This refers to the regular care of fixtures and fittings on the premises, both internally and externally, so that as soon as a potential fault is identified it may be dealt with in the appropriate manner, thus preventing many faults actually occuring and causing concern.

Preventative maintenance is carried out by all members of staff in all types of establishment, but the following guidelines will prove helpful for all:

- *Look* – for any change in colour, shape, texture, performance.
- *Listen* – for any change in sound of any mechanisms.
- *Check* – for any damage or inability to achieve standard required.

In the housekeeping department, likely areas of preventative maintenance could include any of the following:

- Plumbing – taps dripping, drains slow to clear, overflows blocked.
- Floors – frayed areas, stains, bare patches, uneven areas.
- Windows – loose fitting frames, broken catches or sash chords, cracked glass.
- Doors – loose fitting, ill fitting knobs, faulty locks, door catching floor.
- Furniture – chipped, stained, cracked, castors stuck, shelves warped.
- Fittings – curtain rails loose, shelves unsafe, pictures unsteady.
- Electrical – light fittings loose, flickering lights, clocks unreliable.
- Equipment – unreliable, not working efficiently, noisy, flex frayed.
- Decorations – Paintwork or wallpaper marked or chipped.

Any faults or potential faults are reported to the duty housekeeper or the supervisor, who will then be responsible for the assessment of the fault and for reporting it to the maintenance department or contractor for repair.

Regular maintenance

This means that a complete check is made of every single item in a given area at regular intervals. The housekeeper will instruct her supervisors to carry out maintenance checks in each room during a not too busy period. Any faults are recorded on a check-list. The housekeeper will then arrange for the necessary repairs and maintenance to be completed, either by the in-house staff or by contractors. Maintenance check-lists are designed to remind staff of all the furniture, fittings and other items which should be checked.

Some establishments are not open to regular trading all year round, such as holiday hotels at the seaside, boarding schools, halls of residence; these types of establishment can complete their regular maintenance checks and work while they are closed for general trading. Redecoration is often completed when closed or at less busy times of the trading year.

Contract services

Some contract work may be identified in the majority of catering and residential establishments. Contractors may undertake a particular area of work or a definite task, such as window cleaning, at regular intervals throughout the year.

The advantages of contract services
- No capital outlay for equipment.
- No specialist equipment lying idle.
- Trained staff to complete tasks.
- Pre-determined costs.
- Specialist tasks undertaken.
- Extra work done without increasing staff numbers.
- No recruitment/training costs.

The disadvantages of contract services
- No emergency cover available.
- No staff loyalty to the organisation.
- Security risks increased.
- Frequent staff changes.
- Poor liaison between contractors and the organisation.
- Contracts difficult to ammend.
- Little staff supervision by contractor.
- Poorly defined work schedules.

Types of service offered by contractors

Catering
- Cleaning premises.
- Maintenance of equipment.
- Food provision, preparation.
- Equipment hire.
- Food supply.
- Uniform supply/ hire.
- Vending machines.

Housekeeping
- Linen hire.
- Floral decorations.
- Picture hanging.
- Carpet cleaning.
- Toilet – hygiene.
- Vending – sanitary.
- Premises cleaning.

General
- Window cleaning.
- Exterior maintenance.
- Maintenance of grounds
- Equipment hire.
- Factory cleaning.
- Floor maintenance.
- Decorating premises.

Many welfare establishments use contractors for the following types of service:

Schools/universities
- Interior/classroom cleaning.
- Sports ground maintenance.
- Cleaning windows.
- Provision of meals.
- Linen and uniform hire.

Hospitals
- Interior/ward cleaning.
- Staff accommodation cleaning.
- Laundry and linen hire.
- Provision of patients' food and staff meals.
- Vending machines for staff and out patients areas.
- Window cleaning.

Building considerations for guests with special needs

Guests with special needs may require modifications to be made to the average residential building. Guests who are confined to a wheelchair, or who are deaf, elderly, blind or mentally handicapped, do find some hotels impossible to enter and cope with, or at least daunting and unwelcoming. A little forethought and consideration can help to make these groups of guests feel welcome and comfortable.

Main areas

- Wide doors with either a two-way swing or automatic opening to make it possible to enter and leave without ever having to pull the door towards the guest.
- Level or gently sloping access from the exterior parts of the premises to make access possible for wheelchairs and those guests who find walking difficult.
- Hand rails fitted to pathways outside the building as well as inside to make walking about in unfamiliar places easier for the blind guest as well as for those who find walking difficult.
- Signs at entrances placed at a low level for wheelchair-bound guests and signs raised slightly for easy reading by blind guests.

Lifts/stairs

- An adequate number of lifts to the required areas.
- Low call buttons for lifts, with raised signs, to help the blind and those in wheelchairs.

- Wide doors for the lifts with level access, with no gap between the floor and the inside of the lift.
- The interior part of the lift needs to be large enought to turn a wheelchair around, so that the guest can leave the lift safely.
- Strong (low level) hand rails on both sides of the stairs are needed for the elderly and for blind guests.

Bedrooms

- A large space is necessary to enable wheelchairs to be turned around without damaging furniture.
- A low bedside light switch is easier for most guests to use.
- The bed should be the same height as the standard wheelchair.
- The wardrobe should have a low level hanging rail for clothes.
- All cupboards should have sliding doors to make this area less hazardous.
- Televisions should have a remote control facility. An amplified sound facility for the deaf guest is an asset, as other guests are not disturbed by the volume.
- A telephone with press buttons, flashing light signals and an amplifier is a help to all guests with special needs.
- Door numbers need to be raised to enable the blind guest to identify his/her whereabouts. They also need to be large and low enough for the wheelchair-bound guest to read easily.
- The guest information sheets and notices in bedrooms should be printed in Braille and in large print.
- The emergency exits and instructions should be shown to guests upon their arrival.

Toilets/bathrooms

- The entrances need to be wide enough for a wheelchair and to enable the door to be closed easily. The wheelchair will need to be turned around inside the room and placed by the side of the water closet, so adequate space must be provided for these manoeuvres.
- Strong hand rails need to be fitted to help the guests move safely. These may be wall or ceiling mounted.
- The hand basin needs to be fitted at the height most suitable for wheelchair-bound guests. There needs to be knee room below the basin to facilitate its use by those in wheelchairs.
- The taps should be of a design that makes them easy to use by all guests with special needs, for example push design, extended handle design, or mixer taps.

- The toilet needs to have a low flushing handle and a safe, easy-to-lift seat.
- The electrical hot air hand-drier needs to be mounted on the wall at a safe height for those guests in wheelchairs, without them having to stretch up to reach.
- The signs outside the toilet should be clear, and yet not indiscreet.
- The shower unit may be fitted with a seat for the less agile guest to use.

It should be appreciated that if these modifications are instigated in a hotel they will enable a great number of guests both to enjoy and to benefit from their stay; and many of these modifications are not costly to install. When the need arises these rooms can be used by able-bodied guests, so the total hotel occupancy rate will not necessarily be reduced if at any time there are no handicapped guests booked into the hotel. It is often possible to use a twin-bedded room for a handicapped guest by removing one of the beds if required. The only point to watch here is that access into the room must be large enough and access into and inside the bathroom must be adequate for wheelchair-bound guests. Many of the rails and telephone adaptions may be removed when not required.

Work and method study

Work study is the analysis and measurement of work or movement required to perform a task; it is a study of all aspects of work to discover ways of improving efficiency and reducing waste of effort, thereby improving productivity.

Work study examines each aspect of the task and reduces unnecessary movement. Work measurement is the term used to establish how long a task or service should take an operative to perform or complete.

An improved or revised series of stages or steps are devised to enable staff to complete a given task in a more efficient manner. Work study is normally used when management has reason to suspect that its staff are not working in the most efficient manner, for example:

- Staff are becoming slow and overtired, and prone to accidents.
- Staff are unable to complete their work schedule within the allocated time.
- Guests complain of slow or unsatisfactory service.
- There is high staff turnover or staff absenteeism.

Two typical examples can be seen from the following table:

Problem	Cause	Solution
Food service staff overtired, and many minor spillages and accidents occuring.	Staff routes to and from the kitchen are confused and staff are uncertain of the correct way.	By repositioning the furniture and fittings, staff routes can be simplified and clearly defined. Food service staff can go from the kitchen without crossing the service routes in the restaurant.
Excessive tiredness of room service staff. Guests' complaints that early morning calls are late.	Room-maids' service room is at one end of the work area. This makes the distance to be covered very great.	Repositioning of the service room in the centre of the area. Re-allocating the work areas to reduce the amount of walking and the distance from the service room.

The main stages to be followed are outlined below:

1 Identify a problem area or task.
2 Record and analyse existing methods or stages.
3 Identify the trouble areas or stages.
4 Devise new or improved methods.
5 Set a standard to be achieved when using the new method.
6 Implement the new method.
7 Maintain a check on the new method; revise further if necessary.
8 Consult with the staff working the new method at all stages of planning.

Accident prevention

It is essential that all persons employed in the catering industry are capable of using tools and equipment in a manner that will neither harm themselves, those with whom they work, or guests.

Accidents can occur because of staff hurrying around, failure to concentrate on the task in hand, or failure to apply the safety rules.

For example, if staff are hurrying:

- Work may be left before it is properly completed.
- Floor polish may not all be removed, leaving a slippery surface.
- Floors may not be dried adequately after being washed.
- Staff running will cause them to bump into other people.

- Equipment may be used in a casual manner, leaving flexes trailing.

If staff are not concentrating:

- The wrong type of cleaning agents may be used, causing slipperiness.
- Equipment may be left lying around the building, causing people to trip up.
- Electrical equipment may be used incorrectly.

Safety rules are made to protect staff from accidents while they are at work. To comply with the Health and Safety at Work etc. Act 1974 all new staff should be properly instructed in the use of equipment, processes and cleaning agents which they are likely to use while carrying out their job. This instruction should be recorded by the employer. Records of all staff training should be kept up to date and should be available for reference if required,.

Accidents

All accidents to staff or guests should be reported to management immediately. A clear statement of events leading up to and including the accident must be written in the accident book, which should be kept in the manager's office. This report is essential even if the injured person does not appear to be badly hurt. An insurance claim may be filed at a later date and a record of the accident must be available.

Hazards – the following areas should be checked to help prevent fire or accidents.

Residential areas
- Electrical equipment unplugged.
- Television aerial unplugged.
- Floor coverings secure.
- Floor mats lie flat.
- Lighting adequate during day/night.
- Litter and refuse removed.
- Cleaning agents suitably stored.
- Ashtrays emptied.
- Fireplaces guarded.

Outdoors
- Well lit approaches and car-parks.
- Level, safe paths and steps.
- Leaves and debris swept up.
- Delivery areas secure.
- Empty crates and bins suitably stored.
- Outbuildings secure.
- Garages locked, oil and petrol stored.
- Access to and from road well signed.

Fire prevention

Fires may occur in residential establishments and lives could easily be lost if rules are not followed. There are now extensive regulations to cover safety precautions in public buildings to ensure that there is a safe and usable exit in any part of the building in the event of a fire. The local fire brigade has the authority to inspect premises to see that these regulations are being enforced. For more information please refer to the Fire Precautions Act 1971.

Fire doors

These are installed to prevent fire spreading around the building. They should be able to retain the heat of the fire; they should therefore never be wedged open.

Emergency exits

These should be kept clear at all times in readiness for use. Areas in the immediate vicinity should not be used for storage, as this can block exits and could cause a potential fire hazard itself.

Outside fire escapes

These should be kept safe, have strong rails and be well lit at all times. There should be nothing stacked around the ground level area or on any of the stairs or platforms. Empty crates, bins and boxes should not be stacked around/near the base of the fire escape.

Lifts

These should never be used after a fire warning has been called. The lift shaft provides oxygen to all floors and can create a tunnel of flame which easily spreads the fire to other floors if the lift doors are opened. All lifts should return automatically to the ground floor and be rendered inactive when the alarm bell is set off. Lift shafts are usually enclosed to their full height with fire resistant material, and they are usually fitted with fire resistant doors on all floors.

Here are two examples of fire drill procedures.

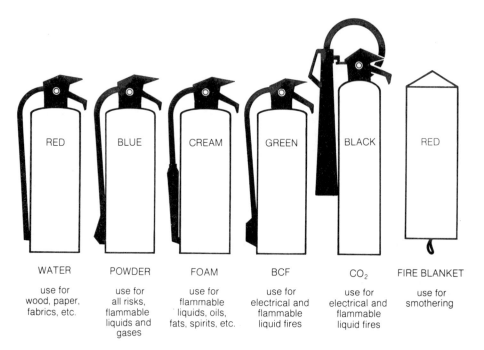

WATER	POWDER	FOAM	BCF	CO$_2$	FIRE BLANKET
RED	BLUE	CREAM	GREEN	BLACK	RED
use for wood, paper, fabrics, etc.	use for all risks, flammable liquids and gases	use for flammable liquids, oils, fats, spirits, etc.	use for electrical and flammable liquid fires	use for electrical and flammable liquid fires	use for smothering

The different types of fire extinguisher

Hotel fire procedures

Because the guests in a hotel can change daily there should be clearly laid down procedures for all guests to read and follow. A clearly printed card for each bedroom and public area should give precise instructions as to the fire drill procedures and the nearest emergency exit. Staff must show these instructions to guests when they are first taken to their rooms. Fire alarm bells should be installed in easily accessible places on advice from the local fire brigade.

In the event of a fire

The receptionist, night porter or front office manager should take the hotel register to check the occupants of the hotel. The fire brigade should be automatically called. Senior residential staff should check the vacancy of an allotted number of rooms and escort guests out of the hotel. Windows should be shut but not locked. All guests and staff should be marshalled to a safe place away from the buildings

126

where they can be given shelter and where the hotel register can be checked. Staff should have regular fire drill practices and instruction so that they all know exactly what they are required to do in the event of a real fire.

In the event of a bomb scare/alarm
All persons should be evacuated from the building as for a fire alarm, with staff being responsible for an allotted section of the building. Usually, this is a different sounding alarm than for a fire. If possible, occupants should take hand luggage with them as they evacuate the building. All doors and windows should be left open. All persons should be marshalled well away from the premises to a place of shelter and safety, where the register should be checked. No person should be permitted to re-enter the building, or to stand anywhere near it until the entire premises have been declared safe by the police and the bomb disposal squad. This can take a considerable length of time, and it is the staff's responsibility to ensure that the hotel guests are kept together and kept as calm and comfortable as possible until further temporary arrangements can be made.

Fire procedure in a residential school/college

- The warden will have a complete list of the occupants. This list should be removed if the fire alarm is raised, so that the residents may be checked.
- All staff will have a number of rooms to check and will be responsible for escorting the people in these rooms out of the building. Senior students may be elected as additional fire wardens in schools and halls of residence.
- Fire practices should be carried out regularly at various times of the day and night, at meal times and at weekends.
- All persons should know where the nearest emergency exit is situated and the assembly point location, so that they can be checked against the residential list.
- The school or college is responsible for the residents and as some pupils are very young, frequent practices are essential to foster confidence.

The information on the following two pages is from a leaflet 'Help yourself to Gas Safety', produced by British Gas.

Laws about gas safety

There are laws about gas safety. They impose specific responsibilities on those who supply gas, on those who install gas appliances **and on those who use them.** The Gas Safety Regulations are concerned with the individual user's safety.
But they also exist to protect the general public.

Under the Regulations:

- no-one shall use, or let anyone else use, any appliance they know or suspect, to be dangerous.

- only competent people shall install or service appliances or systems. You must not do it yourself if you are not competent. Under the terms of the Gas Safety Regulations, it is illegal for anyone to tamper with pipes, meters or fittings belonging to British Gas.

- you must turn off your main gas supply if you suspect a gas escape;

- you must tell your local gas service centre immediately if an escape continues after you have turned off the main supply;

- you must not turn on the gas, or any appliance, again until the escape or the appliance has been repaired.

    These are points of law and if they are broken, you could face a fine of up to £400.

Labels to look for when buying gas appliances

When you are buying a gas appliance, always look to see that it carries one of these labels:

BSI/QAC Safety Mark   British Gas Seal of Approval

These labels are your guarantee of that type of appliance having satisfied stringent safety requirements and production standards.

128

British Gas 'Seal of Service'

At British Gas we know that you will be looking for guarantees on other aspects of new appliances as well as safety—performance, efficiency, durability, ease of installation, supply of spare parts and so on. So, before we will sell any appliance through our showrooms, our laboratories ensure that the type is satisfactory in all these aspects as well, and the appliance is awarded our 'Seal of Service':

This additional label is your guarantee on any appliance we sell. It lasts a full year and also guarantees any installation work we do. It does not take away any of your rights at law. Extended warranties may also be available for certain new appliances.

Assessment activities

1(a) Write a cleaning work schedule for a room of your choice.
 (b) List the equipment necessary to clean the room.
 (c) Follow the work schedule to clean the room.

2(a) Write a daily cleaning schedule for a hotel bedroom with a bathroom.
 (b) Incorporate the weekly cleaning tasks into your basic daily schedule.

3(a) Design a room inspection form for a room that you use at your place of work or training.
 (b) Use your form when inspecting the room for standards of cleanliness.
 (c) Discuss your findings with other members of your group.

4(a) Look around the premises where you are trained or employed and note any special provisions that have been made/fitted for people with special needs.
 (b) Make recommendations for further improvements to increase the provision of access to and around the pemises.
 (c) Design a wall chart to illustrate your findings to the rest of your group.

5(a) Find out about the fire drill procedures at your place of work or training.
 (b) Follow the fire practice procedures and then analyse your actions and those of others in your group.
 (c) Review the drill procedures incorporating any alternatives or alterations that you feel are necessary from your observations.

Unit 7:

Hotel Reception

The hotel foyer

The purpose of the hotel foyer is to:

- create the atmosphere for the whole premises,
- give a good first impression of the hotel – the first few seconds are vital,
- be welcoming to guests by creating a calm efficient atmosphere.

The functions of the foyer can be seen in the following table.

Function		Examples
To give information about:	• facilities on the premises.	Hairdresser. Health Club. Restaurant. Entertainments.
	• local places of interest.	Historical sites and buildings. Festivals and excursions.
	• local public facilities.	Theatres. Discos. Markets.
To create sales of:	• rooms and suites.	Full or half-board terms.
	• tour and group bookings.	Full or half-board. Entertainments. Excursions, tour guides.
	• functions.	Catering facilities. Licensed bar. Accommodation requirements.
To exercise security:	• during the day.	Full view of all persons entering and leaving the premises. All guests required to sign the register.
	• during the night.	Night porter checks entire premises. Books in/out early/late guests.
	• concerning keys.	Guests' keys controlled and issued.

When a guest enters a hotel foyer he or she may be made to feel welcome – or, unfortunately, they may be made to feel unwelcome and insecure. This feeling of being unwelcome can make a lasting impression on a guest, which is difficult to eradicate. The following situations in a hotel foyer can make a guest feel unwelcome.

- Lighting – poor, dull, shady reception and lounge area.
- Heating – cold and draughty, or hot and stuffy atmosphere.
- Ventilation – stale air and lingering unpleasant odours.

- Space – large, empty or crowded, with many guests milling around.
- Staff – not easily and instantly identifiable by the guest, or not available to greet the guest.

The front office

Front office is the name given to all offices concerned with the booking of rooms and facilities within a hotel.

The reception desk

As this is the first area with which guests will come into contact, their impression of the hotel will be formed by the skill and behaviour of the receptionist on duty. It is therefore essential to have a warm welcome for all guests and members of the public, without displaying undue familiarity, impatience or tiredness. Good manners, patience, quiet efficiency, tact and a positive helpful approach are essential qualities for a hotel receptionist.

Positive helpful approach
- Facial expression – keen, interested.
- Posture – upright, positive.
- Appearance – clean, neat, tidy.
- Speech – clear, direct.
- Time – unhurried, efficient.
- Attitude – helpful.

Unhelpful negative approach
- Facial expression – negative, scowl.
- Appearance – unattractive, scruffy.
- Posture – poor, slouching.
- Speech – unclear, dull, slow.
- Time – slow; keeps guests waiting.
- Attitude – preoccupied, bored.

Guests are pleased and receptive to the facilities and accommodation that the hotel has to offer. They are unlikely to complain if just one small item is not to their satisfaction.

Guests are dissatisfied and unreceptive to the hotel and its staff, making them far more likely to complain about their stay at the slightest provocation.

Close co-operation between all departments of the hotel is essential to the success of the business and the comfort of guests.

```
                    GENERAL MANAGER
                           |
                 ASSISTANT/DUTY MANAGERS
                           |
                  FRONT OFFICE MANAGER
```

Entrance	Reception	Key desk	Cash office	Bill office	Reservations
Concierge	Receptionist	Hall Porters	Cashiers	Clerks	Clerks and telephonists
Welcomes guests as they come into the hotel.	Books guest into hotel. Hotel sales. Direct guest contact.	Allocation of keys. Taking guests' messages.	Monetary transactions. Cash control.	Daily hotel sales. Guests' accounts.	Advances sales reservations. Telephone calls. Hotel sales.

Summary of reception procedures

When *checking in* guests, the following procedure should be followed:

Stage 1 Greet the guests and check their names and reservation details in the diary; if they are a chance booking, ascertain the vacancies on the room status board.

Stage 2 Ask the guests to register in the registration book or on a registration card.

Stage 3 Check that their room is ready for occupation by looking at the room status board, then call a porter. Complete the guests' key card.

Stage 4 Check the guests' registration, and the length of their stay Inform the guests of the tariff details. Ask if the guests have any questions.

Stage 5 Ask the porter to take the guests to collect their key and to take them to their room.

Stage 6 Complete the registration of the guests, reservations chart and room status board.

Stage 7 Pass details to the billing office, so that the guests' account may be opened.

When *checking out* guests, the following procedure should be followed:

Stage 1 Make sure that all last minute charges have been entered onto the guests' account, such as breakfast, telephone calls and newspapers.

Stage 2 Present the final account to guests and receive payment.

Stage 3 Call a porter to collect the key and to take guests' luggage.

Stage 4 Thank the guests and bid them farewell.

Stage 5 Delete guests' names from the departure list. Adjust the room status board.

R – reassurance; the guest is in unfamiliar surroundings.

E – eye contact with the guest.

C – courtesy towards the guest at all times.

E – even-toned, pleasant voice.

P – patience at all times, even on the telephone.

T – tact; displayed when dealing with guests.

I – interest shown in guests' questions and requests.

O – organised; the front office is a vital link within the hotel.

N – neat; at all times while on duty.

I – informative; a knowledge of the hotel facilities is essential.

S – smart in appearance; uniforms should be well cared for.

T – Tidy; charts and other documents must be tidy and legible.

The hotel receptionist

Personal attributes

- A pleasant voice to attract the guest.
- Clear, concise way of speaking to ensure correct information is given.
- Clean, neat and tidy appearance to enhance the hotel's image.

Qualities of the receptionist:

with respect to
GUESTS

- Patience displayed when dealing with guests' requests.
- Politeness towards all the guests.
- Interest shown in the guests and their problems/ questions.
- Sympathy shown towards guests' anxiety or concern in unfamiliar surroundings.
- Knowledge of the surrounding area and of the facilities, both in the hotel and outside, e.g. town, transport, entertainment.

with respect to
MANAGEMENT

- Honesty when dealing with money and stock.
- Logical when dealing with bookings and charts/systems.
- Methodical when working in the hotel system.
- Sensible – the ability to exercise common sense.
- Numerate – able to cope with figure work and cash accurately.
- Literate – able to read and write to an acceptable standard.
- Salesman – able to sell the

- Helpful attitude displayed towards guests at all times.
- Friendly smile for guests at all times.
- Sincerity – a genuine, caring attitude shown.
- Observant – able to anticipate guests' needs and requests.

facilities to the public/guests.
- Flexible – able to work within a team of staff.

Dealing with complaints

- Find somewhere quiet to speak to the complainant.
- Seat the complainant down on a comfortable chair.
- Ask for the *actual* fact or action which has caused the complaint.
- Encourage the complainant to analyse exactly what has caused him/her to become upset – it may not be the hotel's fault.
- Always deal with complaints promptly; never act in a hurry, and keep calm.

Stay calm	Care	Complete facts	Conclusion	Consequences
Keep an even-toned voice. Listen.	Show that you care about the complainant.	Ascertain the actual and complete facts from all sides/persons.	Is this complaint valid? Who/what is responsible?	Are there likely to be any further repercussions? What further action is necessary now?

Hotel reservations

Advance reservations are normally all those that are made at least three days' prior to the date of arrival to allow time for a letter of confirmation and a deposit to be sent.

Hotel reservations can be made in a variety of ways, as shown in the following table.

Telephone request or central reservations office request.	Letter Telemessage Telex	Personal hotel booking or agent booking.	Travel agent booking
1 Booking form 2 Chart booking 3 Complete diary 4 File booking form 5 Await confirmation.	1 Chart booking 2 Complete diary 3 Reply to confirm 4 File letter and reply	1 Booking form 2 Chart booking 3 Complete diary 4 File booking form	1 Voucher received 2 Chart booking 3 Complete diary 4 File voucher

A booking form (see below) ensures that all the necessary information is recorded by acting as a check-list for the receptionist.

```
MR/MRS/MISS _____    ARRIVAL DATE _____

ADDRESS _____    TIME _____ AM/PM

     _____

TELEPHONE _____    NO. OF NIGHTS _____

ROOM   SINGLE _____ DOUBLE _____ NO. OF PERSONS _____

       TWIN _____ SUITE _____ RATE _____

REMARKS _____

     _____

TO BE CONFIRMED      YES _____     NO _____

ACTION TAKEN                         SIGNATURE _____
       DIARY _____     CHART _____
```

The guest should always be informed of the rate that is quoted and filled in on the booking form. The guest should be made aware of what this rate includes, as follows:

Separate charges Accommodation charged per night. All other services are charged as they are used.
Continental plan Combined accommodation and breakfast charge. Guests should be aware that this is normally continental breakfast.
En pension Fully inclusive terms. Demi pension are half-board terms.

Reservation diary

One page/sheet is used per day (see example below). It gives information about the daily bookings.

Date _8th August 1986_   Day _Friday_

Name	Room type	Rate	Date booked	Notes	Room No.
B.R. Black	T/B	£33	22.6.86	near lift	
Mrs A.C. Green	S/B	£30	24.6.86		
Mr & Mrs G Cation	D/B	£38.50	1.7.86	facing back	

As guests book into the hotel their reservation is checked with the diary and the terms are clarified. The room number is allocated and their registration completed.

Reservation chart

When a guest has registered, the reservation/occupancy is recorded on the conventional reservation chart (see below). It is inked into the chart to indicate the guest's arrival/stay. When rooms are allocated provisionally, this is pencilled into the chart.

Month _April_   Year _1986_

Room	Date 1	2	3	4	5	6	7	8	9	10	11	12	13	(to end of month)
401 T/B														
402 T/B			←	Bludell		→								
403 D/B	Ace ↔		Tell ↔											
404 S/B		←		Higgins			→							
405 T/B														

The chart shows that room 402 is twin-bedded and is booked for 3–7th April in the name of Bludell. Room 403 is double-bedded and booked for the night of 1st April in the name of Ace and for the

138

night of 3rd April in the name of Tell. Room 404 is a single room and is booked in the name of Higgins for the 2nd to the 8th April. This type of chart provides an easy guide to room occupancy. It is never inked in until the guest has actually arrived and registered into the hotel.

The hotel register

The hotel is required by law to record the full name and address of every guest over the age of 16 years who stays in the hotel. A hotel register is used for this purpose.

Date	Name	Nationality	Address	Room	Car Reg. No.
19.2.86	George Black	British	5, Hill Top, Barnsley	417	ABS 132 X
19.2.86	Jane Read	British	44, High St, Leith	404	–
19.2.86	Andrew Whyte	British	246, Valley Rd, Bristol	215	DET 348 C
19.2.86	Susan Whyte	British	as above	216	–
19.2.86	Charles Brown	British	6, The Paddocks, Bath	365	GTH 486C

Hotel registration cards

Registration cards are used in large, busy hotels, as the information may be processed as soon as the cards have been completed by the guest at the reception desk. The cards also enable more than one guest to be registered at the same time. Overseas visitors are required to complete an 'Alien's Form' in addition to the hotel register. This gives details of their passport number, place of passport issue and their next destination.

SURNAME _____ CHRISTIAN NAME _____

ADDRESS _____ FAMILY _____

_____ _____

SIGNATURE _____ DATE _____

To be completed by overseas visitors only

PASSPORT NUMBER _____ PLACE OF PASSPORT ISSUE _____

NEXT DESTINATION _____

Room status

It is essential that the front office department has a complete and accurate record of bedroom availability at all times. Room may be over or undersold unless the receptionist knows exactly what is happening in each bedroom. Is it vacant? Is it being cleaned? Is it being redecorated? (See illustration below.)

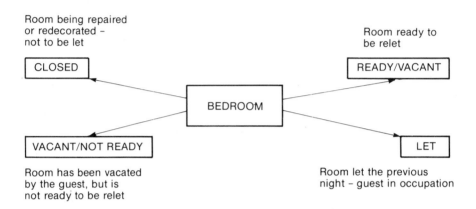

Room status can be recorded by many methods, including the following:

- *Room book*: this system is used in small hotels where the guests leave after breakfast and (usually) the new arrivals do not begin to come in until the middle of the afternoon.
- *Room sheet*: one sheet per day is used to indicate the status of each room on that day. It does not give an instant indication of each room, since the housekeeper uses it in her department. Thus the receptionist has to telephone to enquire about rooms until the daily cleaning is finished at about 3 p.m. each day. Midday and morning arrivals, therefore, can cause delays.

Date 13.2.86 Arrivals					Staying				Departures			
Room	Name	No.	Rate	Dep.	Name	No.	Rate	Dep.	Name	No.	Rate	Dep.
317 TB	Brown	2	£55	16th					Blue	1	£50	13th
318 DB	Black	2	£50	15th								
319 TB					Geat	1	£40	15th				

Mr Blue is departing from room 317 on 13th. Mr and Mrs Brown are arriving to occupy room 317 until 16th, and Mr Geat is in room 319 until 15th.

Density charts

A density chart (see below) is a method of recording in the front office the allocated/let rooms, so that the receptionist can see which rooms are vacant.

Thus the receptionist has picture of the week's lettings at a glance. The rooms are grouped according to their type and are crossed through in pencil as they are let. Group bookings may be ruled through to indicate booking.

MONDAY	TUESDAY	WEDNESDAY	THURSDAY
Singles (25) ØØØØØØØØØØ ØØØØØØØ000 00000	ØØØØØØØØØØ ØØØØØØØØØØ ØØØ00	ØØØØØØØØØØ ØØØØØØØ0000 00000	
Doubles (20) ØØØØØØØØØØ ØØ00000000	ØØØØØØØØØØ ØØØØ000000	ØØØØØØØØØØ ØØØØØØ0000	The chart continues in this way to cover a complete seven-day week at at time.
Twins (30) ØØØØØØØØØØ ØØØØØØ0000 0000000000	ØØØØØØØØØØ ØØØØØØØØ00 0000000000	ØØØØØØØØØØ ØØØØØØØØØØ ØØØØ000000	
Suites (3) Ø00	Ø00	Ø00	
Groups			

From this chart it may be seen that:

- On Monday there are 17 single rooms, 12 doubles and 15 twins booked.
- On Tuesday there are 23 single rooms, 14 doubles and 18 twins booked.
- On Wednesday there are 16 single rooms, 15 doubles and 24 twins booked.

To ascertain which rooms are let/vacant the receptionist will have to refer to the rooming book/sheet, or to the conventional chart if manually booking rooms.

A computerised system will replace the density chart in its usual format and will give readings of the total rooms vacant, the rates per night, and the facilities in each; thus, it is a far quicker system, since it eliminates a complete process.

Manual accounting – tabular ledger

The tabular ledger (see below) is the means used to record all the daily transactions in the hotel. The guest's bill is prepared simultaneously by the clerk in the billing office.

The duplicate slips are sent to the billing office from the various departments in the hotel where the guests have incurred charges. These charge slips are then entered on to both the tabular ledger and the guest's account. Thus both are kept up to date at all times.

There is a new tabular ledger sheet for each day; the daily balances are taken in the late evening and the balances carried forward to the new sheet.

When a guest is due to settle his/her account before departure, the charge slips are checked to ensure that none are omitted from the final bill. The ledger is totalled and the bill is finalised and presented to the guest for settlement.

Upon payment the bill is receipted and the top copy returned to the guest. The carbon copy is filed until the ledger is closed at the end of the day's trading; these copy bills may be needed if there is any query or discrepancy.

The tabular ledger and copy bills are then filed for the accountants and used at a later date.

Room No.	Name	Charge	B/fast	Lunch	Dinner	Liquor	Sundry	Total	B/f	Total	Cash	Credit	Allowances	c/f
362	Black	73.00	4.50	–	8.00	3.50	1.00	90.00	85.00	175.00				175.00
354	Green	73.00	4.50	6.75	7.75	5.10	0.40	97.50	–	97.50	97.50			–

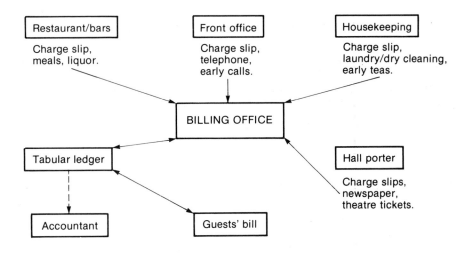

Front office records

Room board

The board is positioned in the front office area and has one slot for each room. When a room is let a card is completed and placed on the board. The cards give the guest's name and the rate to be charged. Coloured cards indicate group bookings.

Different cards denote the status of the rooms, and indicate whether they are ready for letting, being cleaned or already occupied. As with the room sheet and room book systems, this board relies upon good and frequent communication with the housekeeping department.

Computer

The computer has largely taken the place of the room board system, with VDU terminals giving up-to-the-minute information to the housekeeper, front office and duty manager. The print-out facility for hotel recordings and forecasting gives an added advantage over the well established room board, room sheet and room book systems.

Arrivals and departures

A list is prepared from the front office and distributed to the hall porter's desk, the cashier, the billing office, telephonist and housekeeper; they all need to be aware of the names and numbers of guests arriving and departing. A computer VDU will give an instant list, or a print out may be prepared and distributed.

Guest history record cards

Hotels keep records of guests, (see below), so that in the event of a rebooking any information in their previous visit may be used to ensure that their preferences are acknowledged. These records/cards also give immediate access to information about guests with whom the management does not wish to do any further business. The computer VDU will give the same information as the manually kept cards.

Name _____ Tel No. _____					
Address _____					
Remarks					
Arrival	Departure	Room	Rate	A/c paid by	Date paid

These records are very useful for tracing guests who have left property in the hotel, for advertising new business deals, and for remembering guests who call regularly.

Guest facilities

Early morning calls, newspapers, etc.

A card is filled in by the guest and hung on the door handle of the room so that the room-maids are able to collect them and implement the calls as required. These requests are normally made in the evening for the following morning.

Calls are requested from the hall porter's desk by the guests and then at night a list is prepared and distributed for appropriate action in the housekeeping department.

Some hotels have rooms with tea-making facilities and an alarm clock, to provide each guest with their own individual service. When a guest telephones to the front office the call is linked and recorded by computer terminal. The printer will then issue a complete record of all requests for each service section.

Hospitality business club

Companies which have to arrange for their executives and senior personnel to spend nights away from home are encouraged to participate in hotel hospitality schemes. These give preferential rates to companies, and welcome executives personally, thus eliminating lengthy registration procedures at the reception desk. Business/executive rooms and suites are available to these company guests and meeting rooms may be hired, with secretarial services to enable the executives to work in comfortable surroundings.

Space saving and folding furniture is often used to create a variety of uses within the same area, and to maximise the sale of space/rooms. For example, a twin-bedded room can be converted into a small meeting room in the following way:

- beds folded into false wall cupboard,
- wall table unit extended to create larger meeting table,
- arm-chairs and coffee tables removed,
- upright chairs placed in the room,
- coffee/refreshment facilities placed in the room.

A hotel suite can be converted into a private meeting suite in the following way:

- bedroom converted as above to create meeting room,
- lounge fitted with mobile refreshment bar/buffet,
- coffee filter machine filled and placed in the room.

When the meeting is finished the room may be quickly and easily converted back to its original state and use. This will mean additional cleaning by the evening shift room-maids is necessary but will have the advantage of creating an additional saleable area overnight, either to one of the guests who was attending the meeting during the day or to a completely different person. Maximum use of all saleable rooms must be maintained.

Methods of payment

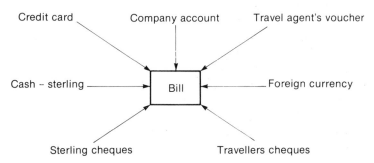

145

Cash sterling

- The best method for the hotel, since the cash is instantly available for use.
- If in large amounts, it can cause banking difficulties and security problems.
- Coins are heavy and bulky.

Sterling cheques

- Banker's cheque cards will guarantee cheques up to £50 in value. This may restrict the use of cheques for guests not known to the hotel.
- The cheque should be signed by the guest in front of the receptionist.
- The cheque card should be valid by date and signature.
- The cashier or receptionist should write the cheque card number on the reverse side of the cheque.
- The cheque itself should be correctly written and the completed figures should agree with the written cash amount.
- Cheques take three days to clear through the bank, thus depriving the hotel of its monetary value until it has been cleared.

Credit card

- Bank credit cards are available to bank customers. The card is used to purchase goods or to pay for services.
- A sales voucher is signed for the total amount of the bill. The bank then undertakes to debit the hotel's bank account with the amount of money paid by the credit cards, minus a small commission charge.
- The cashier takes an imprint of the credit card and obtains the guest's signature upon the triplicate sales voucher.
- The cashier may obtain telephone authorisation to verify the guest's creditworthiness for use of the credit card.

Entertainment and travel cards

- The procedure for accepting these cards and checking the creditworthiness of guests are similar to those for bank credit cards.
- The sales vouchers are sent to the card company at regular intervals. The card company then sends a cheque to the hotel for the amount of the total number of vouchers, minus a small commission charge.
- The time that the hotel has its money tied up in these vouchers may amount to weeks; this is therefore a distinct disadvantage to its cash-flow figures.

Company accounts

- Regular guests from companies who have arranged to have a ledger account with the hotel may simply sign their bill upon departure.
- The hotel will then send the bill to the company, who in turn will settle the account with the hotel.
- The main purpose of this facility is to encourage regular business and executive guests, whose employers will settle their hotel bills.

Travel agent's vouchers

- The travel agent issues a voucher to guests upon receipt of the cost of their intended stay or visit.
- Therefore, when guests arrive at the hotel the voucher is presented as full payment for the agreed services, such as bed and breakfast terms or half-board.
- Care needs to be taken to ensure that all extra services are paid for by guests.
- The creditworthiness of the travel agent needs to be checked before the hotel accepts the booking form from the travel agent.

Foreign currency

- Some large hotels will offer guests facilities to exchange their foreign currency for sterling currency. However, the rate will normally be slightly lower than that available at a bank, to cover the hotel handling charges.
- Exchange rates are constantly changing, owing to international market pressures, therefore an exchange rate table is usually displayed in the hotel for the guests' information.

Traveller's cheques

- The customer purchases the cheques in his own country before commencing his journey.
- They may be in any currency that the customer requires; that of his own country or sterling.
- The traveller's cheques are signed when they are purchased and the serial number's noted by the issuing bank.
- When using traveller's cheques to pay an account, the guest should sign and date each cheque. The cashier should watch the guest sign the traveller's cheques and ask for proof of the guest's identity.
- The traveller's cheques are exchanged for their sterling value by the bank and then credited to the hotel's account.

Billing

Customers' accounts may be prepared manually, mechanically with the aid of a billing machine, or by computerised system:

A summary of the differences between the three systems can be seen in the following table.

Manually	Mechanically	Computer
Tabulated ledger	Electro-mechanical billing machine	Automatically calculated
1 No errors possible, since ledger is balanced vertically and horizontally at the end of each day's trading.	1 The machine is balanced at the end of each staff shift, so errors may be rectified as they occur.	1 Print outs and visual checks are available at any time, in the duty mananger's office and front office as well as the billing office.
2 Extra charges are added by hand, and detailed filing of charge slips is necessary, as cross checking may be necessary.	2 Extra charges are added to the bills at specific times at the end of the staff shift. New balances are automatically given after each charge.	2 Very quick and easy to add on any extra charges, as the keyboards are in each department.
3 A slow method of keeping guests' accounts; only for small hotels.	3 Suitable for a small hotel where guests do not all wish to settle their accounts at the same time.	3 A quick and reliable method of keeping guests' accounts. Instant access to balances and cash queries. VAT is added on automatically.
4 A time-consuming task for a skilled clerk or bookkeeper. Errors are slow to trace.	4 Trained staff are required, and training by specialists is necessary. Correction of errors is a skilled task.	4 Minimum staff needed, but detailed staff training and supervision is essential in all departments of the hotel.
5 Provides a permanent, written record of all trading, although these figures are only partially analysed.	5 Provides a carbon copy of all accounts and charges, but these are not fully analysed.	5 Print outs may be filed to produce permanent records of trading, which have already been analysed.

Safe-deposit boxes

Some hotels offer guests the use of individual safe boxes sited in the cashier's office area of the hotel. Here, guests may have the exclusive use of a safe box to deposit any valuables such as airline tickets, passports, foreign currency and travellers cheques. This facility is required under the Hotel Proprietors Act 1956.

Some luxury hotels have now installed individual room safes in guests' rooms; these are made from electrically welded steel and are anchored to the wall or floor with four steel bolts. They are locked with steel bolts into a solid frame. Guests are provided with the room safe key when they are booked into the bedroom or suite. This system is preferred by guests, since it eliminates the necessity to queue up at the cashier's desk whenever there is a need to get to their safe box. The provision of room safes is an added item to include in the marketing of the rooms, as many guests now expect this provision to be available.

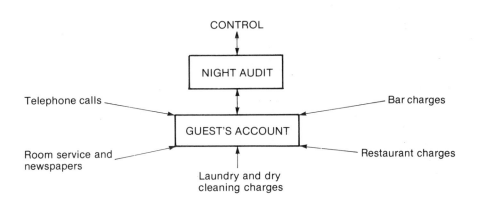

The night audit will check the charges against the guest's account and therefore prepare up-to-date bills ready for the morning.

The daily trading analysis forecasts the next day's trading.

Stock levels are read and reorders prepared.

The use of a computerised system make this auditing and control check far easier, quicker and more accurate. It is one of the main advantages of installing a computerised control system in any business.

Hotel keys

Security of keys

In all cases regular checks should be made on the movement of, and security of, key suites in hotels. Most common losses arise among room keys – thus it is necessary for the front office to keep a reserve set of barrels for interior door locks, so that rooms may continue to be let. Replacement door locks and reissuing of keys should be under the supervision of the security officer or manager.

Key suites are for the opening and locking of guests' accommodation and comprise the following types of key.

Room keys
These are issued by the front office to guests and used by guests during their stay in the hotel to gain access to their rooms. They should be handed in to the front office when guests leave the hotel building or when they check out/depart.

Submaster
These are issued daily to the room-maids at the beginning of their shifts. They enable the room-maid to gain access to all the rooms within her section. The submaster key is returned to the housekeeper at the end of each shift.

Floormaster
This key is issued to the floor supervisor/housekeeper, who has the reponsibility for checking the rooms on that floor. It will open all the doors on that floor.

Grandmaster
This is held by the management level of staff and used to gain access to any room for supervisory or emergency use. The grandmaster key will double lock any room in the case of an emergency.

Loss of the grandmaster key means that no room is secure, therefore strict control of such keys is essential.

Supply keys
These are keys necessary to open such areas as service rooms, storage rooms, cupboards within departments and handed in at the end of the working shift. These keys should never be taken off the premises because of the value of the stock/equipment involved.

Guest key card
A key card is issued to each guest as he/she registers in the hotel. It is used as a means of guest identification, and means that staff can identify any guest as genuine by asking to see the guest's key card.

The appropriate room key will only be issued upon receipt of this card (see below).

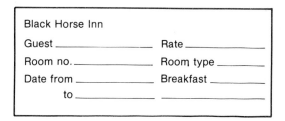

General information advertising the hotel facilities is printed on the reverse side of the card.

The guest key card

Electronic keys

These take the form of plastic key/cards that have a unique lock combination which is changed with the arrival of each guest. They create a secure room without the trouble of replacing lost conventional keys.

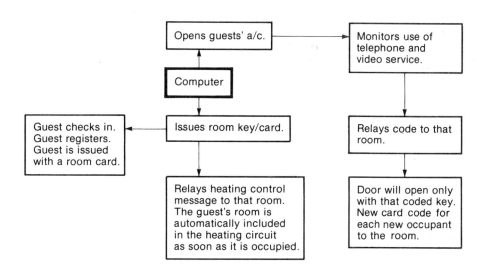

The electronic key is placed in a slot-type lock on the door to the guest's room; when it is correctly placed into the lock the door will unlock.

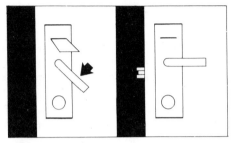

The door is opened by
inserting the keycard in
the slot and depressing
the lever handle.

The door locks auto-
matically when the
door is closed.

The door is deadlocked
from the inside with
the thumb turn.

Both the deadbolt and
latch bolt are simulta-
neously retracted with
the inside lever handle
for immediate exit.
Panic opening.

A double locked door
can only be opened
from the outside with
the emergency key.

An electronically operated key card lock

Assessment activities

1(a) Design a hotel foyer area and illustrate your design with a plan of the foyer and a sketch of the final effect.
 (b) Explain what effect you have been trying to create.

2　Mr and Mrs Blake wish to book a weekend break at a hotel. They have three children: a boy aged 13, a girl aged 7 and a girl aged 7 months; they also have a dog.
 (a) Write a letter to the hotel asking for information (from Mr Blake).
 (b) Write a reply letter from the hotel to Mr Blake.
 (c) Write a confirmation letter from Mr Blake to the hotel, booking the weekend break.

3(a) Design a hotel booking form and complete this for the Blake family coming to stay on the weekend break.
 (b) Design a hotel register sheet/card and complete this for the Blake family coming to stay at the hotel.

4(a) Design a tabular ledger for the seaside hotel and enter the Blake family's stay on this ledger.
 (b) Write out the final account to be presented to Mr Blake at the end of the family's stay.

5　Explain the importance to the hotel receptionist of room status information.

Unit 8:

Management and Business Affairs

The manager

The manager is the leader of the team of staff and the decision maker for the business. He takes the responsibility for the success or otherwise of the business.

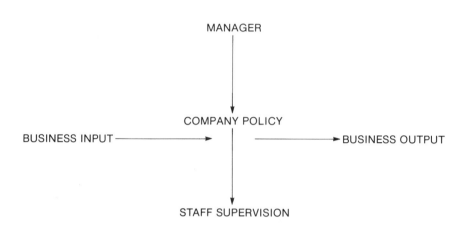

The *qualities* of a successful manager will include the ability to:

- select suitable staff,
- supervise/organise teams of staff,
- predict business trends,
- control financial aspects,
- make valid business decisions,
- use his/her own discretion,
- interpret sales analysis data,
- communicate effectively,
- set and keep to business targets,
- delegate tasks to subordinates,
- comply with relevant legislation.

The *personality* of a successful manager will include:

- willingness to accept responsibility,
- a firm, positive attitude,
- an unbiased attitude,
- an air of authority,
- a respectful regard for others,
- politeness to all persons,
- the ability to work with people,
- a caring attitude towards others,
- a sense of humour in a crisis.

Duties of managers

Hotel manager	Front office manager	Food and beverage manager
1 Control of the business.	1 Control of reservations.	1 Food and beverage sales.
2 Financial control.	2 Sales of facilities.	2 Planning of functions.
3 Marketing and sales.	3 Customer relations	3 Provision of food.
4 Sales analysis.	4 Customer accounts.	4 Service of beverages.
5 Creation of comfortable, inviting establishment.	5 Creates the right image of the business.	5 Control of stock – food and alcohol, tobacco.

House services manager	Domestic services manager
1 Cleanliness of the premises.	1 Control of hospital cleanliness.
2 The maintenance of the premises.	2 Liaison with infection control committee.
3 Maintenance of hygiene.	3 Maintenance of hygiene.
4 Creates an inviting atmosphere.	4 Disinfection and sterilisation of equipment.

Staff motivation

The **manager/supervisor** instructs/asks staff to complete a particular task.

Question: Do the staff
- appreciate the reason for the task?
- have the necessary equipment to complete the task?
- have the knowledge and skill to complete the task?

Answer: *yes* – Staff will be motivated to complete the task.

Upon completion, staff will have the satisfaction of knowing that the task has been adequately completed.

Therefore – **staff motivation** = staff who possess enthusiasm and commitment to the employer and who will complete tasks as requested.

To ensure that members of staff are enthusiastic and committed to the organisation where they are employed, they must be able to:

- feel that they belong to a team of staff in a secure job,
- realise how important and necessary their job is in relation to the rest of the organisation,

- appreciate the consequences of their job and its timing in relation to the rest of the team of staff,
- use their knowledge and skill to their full potential,
- see a clear progression path for their career, and recognise that promotion may be earned,
- use the necessary equipment in a safe and efficient manner,
- complete the job in the required time and to the required standard,
- gain job satisfaction upon completion of the task and recognise a completed job well done.

Factors which enhance staff motivation include the following:

- a pleasant, clean and cheerful work-place,
- a positive attitude displayed by the supervisory staff,
- recognition of the employees' skill, by means of status or financial reward,
- an effective method for employees to discuss their grievances with their employer,
- an effective staff welfare scheme and adequate staff facilities available at the work-place.

Travel agents

Co-operation between hotel management, local authority and travel agents is essential if the full marketing potential of the hotel is to be realised. They are dependent upon each other in the ways illustrated below.

TRAVEL AGENT

★ Makes hotel bookings for the guest
★ Sends confirmation form to the hotel
★ Collects pre-payment from the guest
★ Issues voucher to guest for his stay in the hotel

GUEST ARRIVES AT THE HOTEL

★ Guest stays at the hotel
★ Guest presents voucher for payment
★ Guest pays for any 'extras' (e.g. meals, telephone)

GUEST DEPARTS

★ Hotel sends voucher to travel agent
★ Travel agent pays the hotel after deducting commission

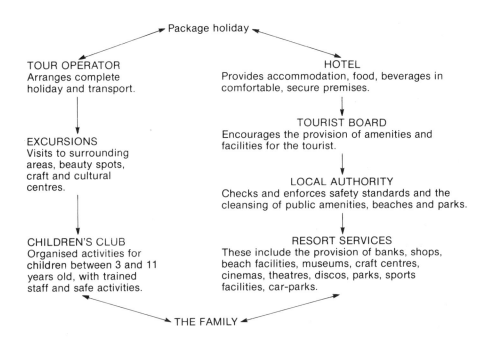

Package holiday

TOUR OPERATOR
Arranges complete
holiday and transport.

EXCURSIONS
Visits to surrounding
areas, beauty spots,
craft and cultural
centres.

CHILDREN'S CLUB
Organised activities for
children between 3 and 11
years old, with trained
staff and safe activities.

HOTEL
Provides accommodation, food, beverages in
comfortable, secure premises.

TOURIST BOARD
Encourages the provision of amenities and
facilities for the tourist.

LOCAL AUTHORITY
Checks and enforces safety standards and the
cleansing of public amenities, beaches and parks.

RESORT SERVICES
These include the provision of banks, shops,
beach facilities, museums, craft centres,
cinemas, theatres, discos, parks, sports
facilities, car-parks.

THE FAMILY

Planning functions

You must aim for maximum use and sales of hotel facilities. On pages 161 and 162 are some examples of facilities which, with forward planning and inter-departmental co-operation, it is possible to arrange.

The hotel management should plan to make maximum use of all rooms that are available for such functions as small private meetings, christening or funeral receptions, wedding receptions and parties, dances, discos, balls, conferences and exhibitions.

The hotel should design its own booking form/system for functions in such a way that the front office staff are reminded to check as many items as possible. The booking form should include the following information:

• Type of room/s required – hire charge, deposit charged.
• Dates (day, month, year) – double check, as frequently booked in advance.
• Time (start and ending) – access times for preparation.
• Catering; types and styles – tea, coffee, alcohol, meals.
• Type of overnight accommodation – for guests who are attending a function.
• Facilities for hire – entertainment, displays, transport, photographer.

Some functions will require specific facilities, such as those listed below:

Wedding receptions

- Food – formal or buffet.
- Drinks – aperitifs, wines.
- Bar – free, limited or cash.
- Cake – style, design, size.
- Flowers – for bride, church, guests.
- Photographer – church, reception.
- Entertainment – evening party, disco.
- Cars – for bride and church reception.
- Accommodation – for guests changing, staying overnight.

Dance/disco/party

- Equipment – music, amplifiers.
- Entertainers – disc jockey, cabaret.
- Special effects – decorations, lights.
- Catering – meals, buffet, beverages.
- Bar – free, limited, cash.
- Drinks – aperitifs, wines.

Conference

- Accommodation – for delegates, staff.
- Meals – before, during and after.
- Transport – to/from airport, railway.
- Refreshments – type, service, style.
- Furniture – seating, tables, dais.
- Display – video, slides, films, flip chart, overhead projector, screens.
- Flowers – colour, display, theme.
- Stationery – pads, pens, blotters.
- Facilities – secretarial, loudspeakers, translators, radio transmission.

Exhibition

- Furniture – tables, stands, dais, screens.
- Facilities – secretarial, translators.
- Communication – telephones, telex.
- Refreshments – for exhibitors, visitors.
- Parking – for exhibitors unloading, cars, coaches, taxis.

Facilities for banquet, dinner dance, cocktail party and reception

Facilities for meetings and seminars, and hotel suites

Sales

It is necessary to determine exactly what facilities are for sale. The following questions need to be considered before any selling takes place.

Personal direct sales

This method of selling is used extensively in all sections of the catering industry. It is simply the staff communicating directly with the general public to create interest in products and facilities, and to effect sales. More details of facilities to be sold and the staff who are able to sell them can be seen in the illustration below.

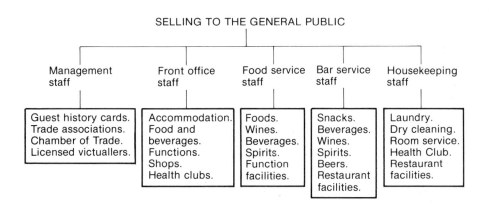

Positive direct selling techniques

It is possible to increase direct sales by adopting positive techniques:

Speech – a clear, even voice should be used, with a pleasant, easy-to-listen-to tone.

Appearance – staff who are clean, neat and tidy, and who have an air of confidence, will help to increase sales.

Attitude – staff who are cheerful, interested and enthusiastic can increase customer satisfaction and, therefore, sales.

Knowledge – staff need an up-to-date knowledge of tariffs, facilities, seasonal bargains and group prices; indecision does not create sales.

Effective selling

Positive phrases may be used to increase sales, as follows:

- 'I look forward to seeing you.'
- 'I look forward to welcoming your group.'
- 'We will be delighted to accommodate you.'
- 'Can I get you anything else?'
- 'Would you like to see the restaurant menu?'
- 'I am sure that you will enjoy your stay.'

Selling food service and house services

The prime objective is to sell these facilities and services to members of the general public and to companies which are likely to use the premises. To achieve this objective it will be necessary to formulate the services offered for sale (see below).

Food and beverage department	House and leisure services
Restaurant – Table d'hote, – A la Carte, – Plat du Jour.	Rooms – single/twin/double suites. Group bookings, tours. Function suites.
Room service.	Additional services – valet, laundry,
Bar snacks and meals.	room service.
Coffee shops.	Hairdresser/barber/manicurist.
Lounge beverage service.	Health and beauty club.
Bar – lounge/public.	Swimming-pool, sauna bath.
– cocktail/lounge.	Sports facilities.
Function catering.	Garage, car-park, coach-park.
Outside/contract catering.	Theatre bookings, adjacent amenities.

A comprehensive booking system is also essential to guard against over or underselling (see below).

To guard against underselling services		To guard against overselling services	
Methods	1 Restaurant booking diary. 2 Function booking diary. 3 Computerised booking sheets.	Methods	1 Front office booking diary. 2 Functions booking diary. 3 Computerised booking sheets.
Tariffs	1 Fixed/standard prices for restaurants and functions.	Tariffs	1 Comprehensive prices. 2 Standard group prices.

Front office sales opportunities

Guest action	Acceptance of minimum sales	Creating maximum sales
Guest telephones to enquire about hotel accommodation.	Telephonist states the room tariffs and the types of room available.	Telephonist describes the room facilities and advantages, then states the tariff.
Guest agrees to accept a room.	Telephonist records guest's details.	Telephonist agrees with the guest's choice, then records the details. Thanks the guest.
Guest arrives and wishes to register in the hotel.	Receptionist records guest's arrival and the registration is complete.	Receptionist greets the guest and promotes the hotel facilities while the registration is being completed. Calls a luggage porter.
Guest collects key from front desk. Luggage porter takes the suitcases.	Luggage porter takes guest to his room, then shows the guest the emergency notice.	Luggage porter takes the guest to his room, shows the guest the emergency notice and details of room service, lighting and heating fittings, telephone and television, and promotes the restaurant facilities.

Guest action	Acceptance of minimum sales	Creating maximum sales
Guest goes to the lounge for a beverage.	Lounge waiter serves guest with the requested beverage.	Lounge waiter greets the guest and pro-motes interest in the foods and beverages by giving the guest a copy of the menu. Serves the guest with the beverage.

From these examples it is possible to appreciate how hotel staff may increase direct sales as they carry out their daily tasks.

For some management teams the minimum sales action may be acceptable but, for the majority of management teams, maximum sales action and the most effective methods of greeting guests is the way staff are expected to work.

It should always be remembered that the guest needs to:

FEEL – welcome,
        secure and at ease,
        comfortable in strange surroundings,
        confident and important in unfamiliar situations.

Staff should work at all times to achieve this.

Sales forecast and analysis

Completed sales are analysed and any slack periods or areas are identified for further advertising and sales. Past sales figures are used to forecast future business trends.

Methods used include analysis of the following:

- Restaurant bookings diary, and restaurant receipts and costs.
- Function bookings, and function receipts and costs.
- Alcohol sales and costs.
- Tour bookings and local forthcoming events.
- Front office accommodation receipts and density chart analysis.
- Future business developments and trends.
- Leisure section receipts and costs.

166

Advertising

There are many ways that a business or facility may be advertised to members of the general public. Firstly, it is necessary to decide:

- which facility or service it is that you wish to promote,
- which precise part of this facility you wish to centre the advertisement upon,
- which media is going to attract the type of business you are hoping to attract/gain.

Types of media

Television
- Expensive, professional expertise is essential.
- Difficult to assess its success.

Newsprint
- Local or national newspapers offer reasonably priced facilities for advertisements, with good coverage.

Magazines
- These may be selected for their specialist readership, covering a particular profession or hobby.

Leaflets
- These may be distributed locally or nationally and have the advantage of an identified coverage.

Billboards
- Professional expertise is essential. It may be difficult to assess success.
- Placed in post offices, on buses, at bus and railway stations, these can be beneficial, since they are local.

One of the best ways to advertise a business is by personal recommendation. To ensure that this applies, it is essential to give each guest such excellent value for money and service that they will recommend your establishment to other people.

Inter-departmental co-operation

Close co-operation within the hotel and between the various departments and sections of the hotel is essential to ensure the smooth running of the business, its success and profitability. There are many methods of communication used in hotels but they all entail the same basic sections and departments (see below).

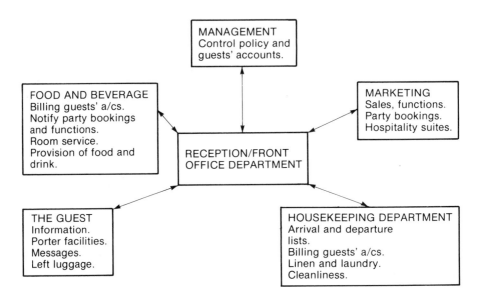

Methods of communication

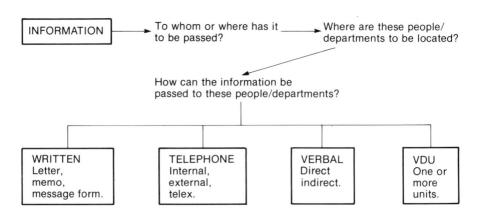

Computers in the hotel

Computers are being increasingly used in hotels for the following tasks/systems:

- customer reservations and billing,
- financial control of the hotel business,
- control of the food and beverage stocks and trade,
- word processing for written communications, letters, and records,
- the logging and billing of telephone calls,
- a complete itemised/sectionalised sales ledger,
- housekeeping, control of stock and room availability.

Adequate expert advice and staff training is essential when a new system of control, information and communication based on a computer is to be installed in any hotel.

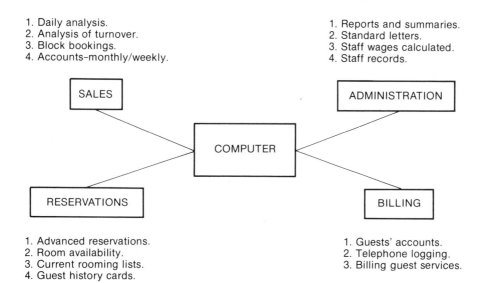

1. Daily analysis.
2. Analysis of turnover.
3. Block bookings.
4. Accounts–monthly/weekly.

1. Reports and summaries.
2. Standard letters.
3. Staff wages calculated.
4. Staff records.

SALES

ADMINISTRATION

COMPUTER

RESERVATIONS

BILLING

1. Advanced reservations.
2. Room availability.
3. Current rooming lists.
4. Guest history cards.

1. Guests' accounts.
2. Telephone logging.
3. Billing guest services.

Banking facilities

The following information on Banking facilities is taken from 'Sample Bank cards, forms and documents' by the Banking Information Service.

Cheques

The first cheque shown is an 'open' cheque, It is called an 'open' cheque because A. Trader can get cash for it from the cashier at the High Street, Caxton branch of Barclays Bank. Another type of cheque – a crossed cheque – is shown below. The purpose of the crossing is to provide a safeguard. A crossed cheque must be paid into a bank account, so a lost or stolen crossed cheque is unlikely to be paid into the account of the person finding the cheque, because it could be traced.

An 'open' cheque can be 'crossed' simply by ruling two lines across the cheque (as shown) but now cheques are often issued with the crossing already printed.

Cheques are supplied by the banks, in book form, for the use of current account customers. On the left hand side is the cheque counterfoil (or stub) which is retained to provide a record of payment.

Notes on completing a cheque
Write clearly. Leave no spaces which could make it easy for somebody to alter the details. Do not carry signed blank cheques.

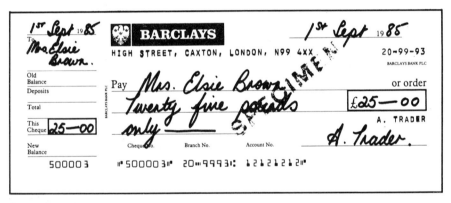

Open cheque

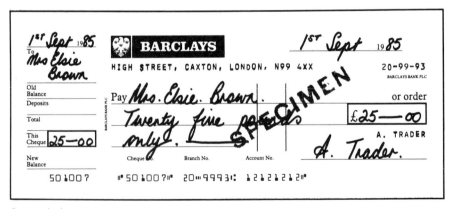

Crossed cheque

170

STOP payment

After Mr. Brown had posted a cheque in payment of an account, he was very surprised when later the account was sent to him again. Upon enquiry he learned that his cheque had never been received and must have gone astray. He immediately contacted his bank and found out that the cheque had not been presented for payment. Mr. Brown therefore gave the bank his authority (below) to stop payment of the missing cheque and to return it unpaid to anyone presenting it. He then issued a second cheque in payment of the account.

The staff of the branch keep a careful watch for the lost cheque among those which are presented for payment. But as a safeguard, a record of the 'Stop' is placed on Mr Brown's computer file. If the cheque is subsequently presented for payment, the computer either automatically rejects the entry or issues a warning to the branch where Mr. Brown has his account.

Example

TO BARCLAYS BANK PLC

HOMETOWN.   BRANCH

NAME OF ACCOUNT

A . BROWN .

*Please **STOP** payment of the undermentioned cheque/cheque book

*Please **CANCEL** all future Direct Debits originated against the undermentioned Mandate

Crossed/Uncrossed
Cheque Number _00659_   Dated _1 AUG 85_   Amount £ _56·62·_   Frequency *(if Direct Debit)* _____

Payee/Originator _A . B . C . Co . LTD ._   Originator's Reference _____

until further instructions are received from me in writing.

CUSTOMER'S SIGNATURE _A. Brown ._   DATE _1 SEPT 85 ._
*Delete as applicable

FOR BANK USE ONLY: *(Initial where appropriate)*

| DATE AND TIME OF RECEIPT | | | WRITTEN CONFIRMATION REQUESTED | | WRITTEN CONFIRMATION NOT REQUIRED | | REMINDER SENT AFTER 7 DAYS | |

ACCOUNT ENTRY ENQUIRY		IF ENQUIRY OR INTERIM UNAVAILABLE CLEARING AND DAY'S WORK EXAMINED *(if applicable)*		NEW CHEQUE BOOK ORDERED *(if lost/stolen)*		**STOP ON (DR AMOUNT)**	
						ORIGINATED BY	DETAILS CHECKED BY
INTERIM LEDGER REPORT REQUESTED *(if applicable)*				LEDGER SHEETS EXAMINED *(if applicable)*			
FATE REGISTER EXAMINED		CHARGE APPLIED		Stops to be recorded on Visible Index		**STOP OFF (CR AMOUNT)**	
		IF AMENDMENT REJECTED OR INCORRECT CHECKS CARRIED OUT AGAIN		STOP STRIP CHECKED AND PLACED IN VISIBLE INDEX		ORIGINATED BY	DETAILS CHECKED BY
SPECIAL PRESENTATIONS FILE EXAMINED							

CODE [ ][ ][ ]   ACCOUNT NUMBER [ ][ ][ ][ ][ ][ ][ ][ ]   SERIAL/ORIGINATOR'S IDENTIFICATION NUMBER [ ][ ][ ][ ][ ][ ][ ]   AMOUNT £ [ ]

130 (7/85)

171

Traveller's Cheque

The traveller's cheque provides a safe and convenient way of carrying money, and is ideally suited to the holiday-maker and traveller.

Traveller's cheques can be cashed not only at the branches of all the main banks in the British Isles but also in most banks abroad and they are frequently accepted at hotels and by large shops.

Anyone can buy traveller's cheques and they are available in denominations of £5, £10, £20, £50 and £100. At the time of purchasing, each cheque must be signed at the foot — where it says 'signature of the drawer'. When presenting for payment, it must be signed again where it says 'Drawer's Endorsement' and dated — in the presence of the paying agent.

It is also possible to purchase traveller's cheques drawn in a foreign currency.

Example

Credit Slip or Paying-in Slip

Here is a credit slip made out by Mr. Brown and ready for handing to the cashier at the bank where his account is kept. As you can see the credit is made up of notes, coin and a cheque. The cashier counts the cash, examines the cheque and checks the credit generally. He then initials it and impresses his counter stamp on the counterfoil and the credit slip. The counterfoil is retained by Mr. Brown as his receipt and as a record of the transaction.

When examining the cheque paid in by Mr. Brown the cashier checks it is payable to Mr. Brown. If not, the cashier will ensure that the original payee has signed his name on the reverse (this is called an endorsement). Example

A Cheque Card

A cheque card is a guarantee by the issuing bank branch that it will pay cheques drawn in association with the card to the extent of £50 for any one transaction. As a means of identification it shows the name and the specimen signature of the holder, the card serial number and the date of expiry. The card may be used:-

a) To enable the holder to encash a cheque up to £50 at any branch of any bank within the scheme.

b) To support a cheque up to the value of £50. Any payees accepting a cheque under the terms of a cheque card, can rely on the cheque being paid, provided the rules governing the use of the card are observed. It is not possible to 'stop' payment of any cheque issued under a cheque card.

Barclaycard

Confusion sometimes arises because a Barclaycard may be used both as a credit card and a cheque card (to guarantee Barclays Bank cheques up to £50).

A Credit Card

This enables the holder to buy goods or services at any shop, restaurant, garage, etc., which has joined the scheme, without paying by cash or cheque at the time of making the purchase. Each shop in the scheme is allotted a 'floor limit' beyond which it cannot accept a credit card in payment for goods without first confirming the transaction by telephone with the credit card company. Also each card holder is given an overall personal limit which cannot be exceeded.

The card is presented and a voucher is signed by the card holder. The supplier sends one copy of the voucher to the credit card company by paying it into his bank account. The card holder retains the original voucher for his records and is presented with a statement at the end of the month showing all the transactions he has made with the card during that month. This account he settles by one monthly payment, thereby saving the necessity of carrying cash around and reducing the number of entries on his bank account and possibly also his bank charges: the account can be paid in full or by instalments at which stage interest will be charged. There are many thousands of shops, garages, restaurants and other places which belong to the scheme and it is possible to do a great part of one's spending in this way. It is however important to keep some record and use the card with discretion.

The card will also enable the holder to obtain cash up to a given limit at any of the branches within the issuing bank's system.

Access card

Postal services

Postal services are a valuable part of business communication and main post offices provide leaflets giving details of all the services that are available and the current charges. A summary of the services that are available for the conveyancing of letters, packages and parcels is shown below.

Type	Service	Uses
First class	Delivery within 24 hrs of posting.	Fast mail, business mail.
Second class	Delivery within 2/3 days of posting.	Routine mail.
Special delivery	Same day delivery – expensive.	Urgent mail.
Express post	Same day messenger service.	Business documents.
Railway post	Collected from one station and delivered to another station.	Fast bulky mail – customer collects from station.
Data post	Overnight delivery of post.	Urgent business mail.
Recorded delivery	Gives proof of posting – receipts.	Postage of documents.
Registered post	Compensation paid for losses.	Valuable items.

Telex service

This service provides a quick means of communicating in printed form with other subscribers, combining the speed of the telephone with the printed word. The printed copy of the message is produced on the teleprinters at both the sending and the receiving subscribers' installations. Calls may be made at any time to any other telex subscriber. Messages may be transmitted to the subscriber even though the teleprinter is unattended, provided it is switched on. The message is then available for attention when the operator returns to the machine. The rental charge covers the provision and full maintenance of the teleprinter, control unit and line to the telex exchange. Companies which subscribe to the telex network are issued with a link number. These are usually displayed with the full address and telephone number on official notepaper headings. There is also a telex directory for subscribers.

Telephone service

This is one of the fastest and most convenient methods of communication between two people in different locations. If a message has to be taken over the telephone it is essential to make a note of all the relevant information. To help staff remember to ask for all the necessary details, most employers use printed message forms. These should be kept by the telephone, together with a pen, so that all messages may be recorded accurately. Messages that are not passed on or incorrectly recorded can be the causes of lost business and trade. Inefficiency when speaking over the telephone can have a lasting damaging effect on future business.

Telephone style

- A clear, concise method of speech should be used when speaking on the telephone.
- An even, slow tone should be adopted.
- Slang expressions should never be used.
- Polite conventional terms and methods of speaking should be used.

Expressions which will create a business-like impression:

- 'Good morning/afternoon.'
- 'Can I help you?'
- 'Please wait a moment.'
- 'I will find out.'
- 'Thank you for calling.'
- 'I will forward the ......'
- 'I will transfer you to . . . . . .'
- 'I look forward to meeting you.'

Expressions which will create an unfavourable impression:

- 'Hello', or 'Hi.'
- 'Yes', or 'OK.'
- 'Hang on', or 'Wait a mo.'
- 'I don't know.'
- 'Cheerio', or 'So long.'
- 'I'll send it.'
- '..... will deal with you.'
- 'See you soon.'

```
+---------------------------------------------------------------+
| MESSAGE FOR:                                                  |
|                                                               |
| Mr/Mrs/Miss _____  |
|                                                               |
| While you were out _____ |
|                                                               |
| Mr/Mrs/Miss _____  |
|                                                               |
| of _____  |
|                                                               |
| Telephone no. _____ Extension _____   |
|                                                               |
|     +------------------------+---+  +------------------+----+ |
|     | Telephoned             |   |  | Please ring      |    | |
|     +------------------------+   |  +------------------+    | |
|     | Called to see you      |   |  | Will call again  |    | |
|     +------------------------+---+  +------------------+----+ |
|                                                               |
| MESSAGE _____  |
|                                                               |
| _____  |
|                                                               |
| _____  |
|                                                               |
| _____  |
+---------------------------------------------------------------+
| Date _____ Time _____   |
|                                                               |
| Received by _____  |
+---------------------------------------------------------------+
```

A telephone message form

Methods of communication by telephone

Radiopaging
- Small paging unit that will bleep when the wearer is required by telephone in their office.
- It may be programmed to receive calls in more than one area to increase its value.
- There may be two different bleep tones to enable two different contact points to communicate with the wearer.
- They are miniature radio receivers that may be placed in the pocket.
- Some paging units have a memory unit, so that they will not bleep during meetings or other inconvenient times when switched off. Memory will then relay the call bleep.

Card-caller telephone
- A punched card is inserted and the number is automatically called/connected.
- Useful when some calls have to be made frequently.

Keymaster telephone
- This type can make and receive calls.

176

- The push button operation gives inter-communication between keymaster telephones.
- Useful in small businesses or offices.

Pay phones
- These may be wall mounted for use by the guests or general public.
- Trolley mounted for use in hospital wards or convalescent homes.
- Portable, with plug and socket termination for use at exhibition halls, conferences and functions.

Telephone calls made by guests in a hotel may be made in one of the following ways:

Pay phone Guest uses the pay phone booth provided in the foyer area.

Room phone Switchboard automatically records the time and duration of the calls made, and the numbers dialled by the guest. The charges are then 'posted' to the guest's account.

Room phone via telephonist The hotel telephonist will connect the guest to the call and metre the charges. The charges are then 'posted' to the guest's account.

Security check list

It is essential for all staff to be aware of the importance of security, and for adequate training time to be allocated to this aspect of their responsibilities. All staff should have well defined areas of responsibility within their work schedules. Staff should be aware of the following:

Exterior
- Outbuildings – adjacent properties, garages, car-parking areas.
- Doors – fire exits, windows, drain pipes, climbing plants.

Reception
- Keys – guest keys, staff keys, key suites.
- Guests – luggage, payment by cheque or credit card.
- Desk – in full site of the entrance door/foyer.

Safe
- Type – siting of the safe, installing at premises, illumination.
- Access – to guests' valuables, which staff able to use?

Staff
- Employment – check references, other employers, previous record.

- Security – staff changing room, lockers, keys, supervision.
- Training – delegated areas of responsibility, training, night staff.

Cash
- Cash floats – checking of, signing for, security of.
- Tills – cashing up, till receipts, till rolls, supervision.
- Vending – machines checked and emptied, location of machines.

Goods
- Delivery area – secure area, checking of deliveries.
- Storage – goods inwards, controlled and issued.

Bars
- Stock – spirits, bottled stock, empties, barrels, snack items, crisps.
- Tobacco – control of stock and sales.

Restaurants
- Tableware – storage and checking of items after use.
- Foods – sauces, accompaniments, fruits, mints, coffee.

Housekeeping
- Linen – bed linen, towels, checking to laundry and returns.
- Equipment – use, storage and issue of cleaning agents.
- Wastage – of fuel, heating, lighting, cleaning agents.

Kitchen
- Foods – economy of use, wastage, staff meals, issue and storage.
- Equipment – storage and checking of after use, fuel usage.

Security is only as good as the staff are prepared to make it; any encouragement to staff should therefore be welcomed by management. The following may help you to remember the most important points.

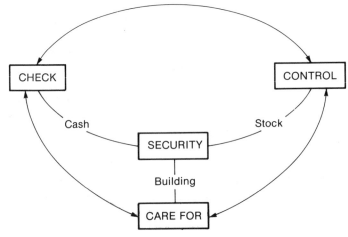

Summary of legislation

The Health and Safety at Work etc. Act 1974

This is in two parts and may be summarised as follows:

a) Legal obligations of employers are:
  • to ensure the health and safety of the employees,
  • to provide a safe area of work, and safe machines, tools and equipment,
  • to provide instruction and training for staff,
  • to write and implement a company safety policy document.

b) Legal obligations of employees are
  • to take reasonable care for his or her own health and safety,
  • to take reasonable care of other people's health and safety,
  • not to misuse any premises or equipment, in the interests of health and safety.

The National Insurance (industrial injuries) Act 1965

This is relevant to all employees. It provides benefit in case of personal injury, industrial disease or death in the course of employment. Any claim must be made within three years of the injury.

Fire Precautions Act 1971

A fire certificate must be granted by the fire authority to all hotels sleeping more than six persons. The certificate ensures that the premises have adequate fire precautions and means of escape, fire resistant doors, fire-fighting equipment and staff training.

Hotel Proprietors Act 1956

Hotels may be liable for the full amount of a guest's loss of property unless a disclaimer notice is permanently displayed near the reception desk where the contract for accommodation is made. All hotel keepers have a duty to exercise reasonable care of all property. The disclaimer notice extends only to property of guests who have engaged sleeping accommodation at the hotel, and is limited to £50 for any one article and £100 to any one guest, except where property has been lodged in the hotel safe. It does not cover loss to motor vehicles or to property left in such vehicles.

A hotel proprietor may refuse to accommodate any traveller whose behaviour or conduct is likely to cause offence to other guests (but not on the grounds of race, nationality, sex, or marital status).

The Race Relations Act 1965

This act makes it an offence to discriminate against any person on the grounds of race or colour.

The Trade Descriptions Act 1968

This act protects the consumer against any false descriptions or statements about goods or services or of conditions which are offered.

The Aliens Order 1953

All persons over the age of 16 years must inform the hotel management of their full name and nationality if staying overnight in the hotel. If the guest is an alien, the passport particulars must be recorded, together with details of his departure date and destination. Records must be retained for at least one year, and must be available at all times.

The Misuse of Drugs Act 1970

The management must not allow its premises to be used by persons who are misusing drugs. Police have the power to search any premises or vehicle when they have reasonable grounds to suspect that a person is in possession of illegal drugs.

The Tourism (Sleeping Accommodation Price Display) Order 1977

This requires all hotels and guest houses to display their tariffs at the reception desk. These charges must indicate exactly what they include, and any service or VAT must be included in the advertised price.

The Dangerous Machines (Training of Young Persons) Order 1954

No person under the age of 18 years may use or work on any of the following machines unless he has received full instruction and training, and is under adequate supervision.

Laundry equipment:
- hydro-extractors,
- calenders,
- washing machines,
- garment presses.

Assessment activities

1(a) Work in a small group with two or three of your colleagues and discuss the term 'staff motivation'.
 (b) Compile a summary of your discussion and present this to the rest of your class.

2(a) Imagine that you are preparing a holiday brochure for a seaside town of your choice.
 (b) List the facilities that you would include in this brochure.
 (c) Design a poster to attract families to visit the seaside town.

3(a) Design a booking form for a hotel function suite.
 (b) List the items that the hotel has for hire.
 (c) Draw a sketch of the hotel function suite.

4 Design an advertisement for a city hotel to be displayed in national newspapers and magazines.

5(a) Analyse the security procedures at your place of work or training.
 (b) Discuss your findings in small groups and write a list of items/areas that you consider to have ineffective security protection.

Index